Instant Vortex Air Fryer Oven

Combo Cookbook

Foolproof, Quick & Easy Air Fryer Oven Recipes for Beginners and Advanced Users

Larry Neary

Contents

SWEETS & DESSERTS RECIPES 49

SNACKS & SIDE DISHES RECIPES 60

VEGETABLES & VEGETARIAN RECIPES 71

FAVORITE AIR FRYER RECIPES 83

INTRODUCTION

Air Fryer

An air fryer is a type of kitchen appliance that air cooks by circulating hot air and minimal or no oil (compared to deep-frying). Most modern air fryers resemble a small box, with a tall stand for the basket and a control panel on top.

The hot air flow generated in an air fryer heats up the food only from the top, leaving the inside of the food moist and tender.

Before we start I think it is important to clear up some misconceptions about the air fryer.

The air fryer is not a deep fryer nor is it meant for frozen foods or ready-made meals alone. An air fryer is everything and more, it can fry, bake, roast and grill and even dehydrate food, in fact, you can boil eggs in the air fryer.

Although some people think this method of cooking eggs is taking things a little bit too far. Well, I can say I agree with them. That said, you can perfectly boil an egg in the air fryer like you would in a pot on the stove or with an instant pot (pressure cooker) without the use of water.

So what is the air fryer good for? It is great for frying chicken, fish, and French fries, pork chops, steak, burgers among other things. It is a great gadget for reheating all types of food, hello Pizza.

Is The Air Fryer Healthy?

The air fryer is not the only cooking method that cooks healthy food. The hype is in the fact that fried foods are very popular and obviously taste better than boiled foods.

Though Deep fried foods like fried chicken, French fries and the likes taste delicious, the draw back is the amount of oil needed to achieve that crispy delicious goodness we all love.

That's where the air fryer fills the gap. The air fryer makes fried foods healthier because it makes fried foods taste awesome with less oil. The method of cooking forcing hot air around the food in such a way that a little oil adds a level of delicious crispiness that can be compared with deep fried chicken. This crispy air fried chicken drumsticks is proof of the how the air fryer makes crispy chicken.

Where Should You Place Your Air Fryer?

Choose an appropriate spot for your air fryer in the kitchen. Always place your air fryer on a leveled, heat-resistant countertop.

Keep it away from the wall. Place your air fryer near the vent hoods and turn them on.

When not in use, you can just pop it in the cupboard and free your counter space. Or move it back closer to a wall or corner in your kitchen.

Before First Use

Open the box and take apart all removable components. Read the Manufacturer's manual included with your appliance.

Before using the air fryer for the first time, remove all of the stickers and plastic packaging from the air fryer.

Setting Up

Place your air fryer on a stable, heat-resistant surface. Keep the air fryer away from any objects or surfaces. This will protect against steam damage.

Take the basket out of the air fryer with the help of a basket release button and separate the inner basket from the outer basket.

Thoroughly clean both baskets by hand washing or in the dishwasher. To dry the basket, use a dry towel. Then, replace the basket in the air fryer.

Tips

1. Before you begin cooking in the air fryer, it can be preheated depending on what you are planning to cook. When preheating your air fryer, the food cooks at a higher temperature and has a crispy exterior. Preheat the air fryer manually for 5 minutes at 400°F. Preheating can be done by clicking the preheat preset button or manually depending on your air fryer.

2. Remove the air fryer basket and place the food in it once the air fryer has finished preheating. However, keep in mind that the basket should not be overstuffed with food. Because overfilling the basket may result in undercooked food.

3. Insert the air fryer basket into the air fryer after it has been filled with food. Then, depending on what you are cooking, set the appropriate time and temperature. The good news is you can change the time and temperature even while cooking.

4. To begin air frying, click the start button. However, once you begin cooking, you must ensure that the food is not overcooked or burned. To ensure that the food is cooked evenly, you can mix/ shake the contents during the cooking process or flip the food. The air fryer will beep once the cooking time is up.

5. After that, remove the air fryer basket. But be cautious of the hot steam. on a flat surface. Before cleaning, the basket must be completely cool.

Poultry Recipes

Air Fryer Butterfly Chicken Drumsticks

 Servings: 3 Cooking Time: 25 Mins.

Ingredients:

- 6 chicken drumsticks
- 1 tbsp. oil
- 1 tsp. paprika
- 1 tsp. Italian seasoning
- 1 tsp. garlic powder
- ½ tsp. onion powder
- ½ tsp. salt
- ¼ tsp. cayenne pepper

Directions:

1. Prepare chicken and split chicken
2. Pat chicken dry. Place on a chopping board and cut on one side starting from the larger side to the thinner end. Open it up so it spreads like a wing.
3. Season the chicken
4. Mix seasoning and salt together.
5. Add oil to butterflied chicken legs then add chicken seasoning blend. Mix till all the chicken is well coated in seasoning.
6. Air fry
7. Transfer seasoned chicken to air fryer basket. Cook at 400°F / 200°C for 25 mins flipping half way through cooking time. Smaller drumsticks will cook in less time. The internal temperature should be at least 165°F / 74°C to be considered fully cooked and safe to eat.
8. Enjoy as is or serve with your favorite side dish. See blog post for suggestions.
9. Oven instructions
10. Preheat oven to 400°F / 200°C / Gas Mark 6
11. Place seasoned chicken on a baking sheet. Bake in preheated oven for 35 to 40 mins or until cooked through and internal temperature reads 165°F / 74°C. Remember to flip chicken half way through cooking time.

Air Fryer Chicken Breasts

 Servings: 4   Cooking Time: 20 Mins.

Ingredients:

- 1 chicken breast (increase accordingly)
- 1/2 tsp. olive oil
- 1/2 tsp. salt
- 1/2 tsp. pepper
- 1/2 tsp. garlic powder (or seasoning of your choice)

Directions:

1. Preheat the air fryer at 180°C (360°F).
2. Brush or spray each chicken breast with oil.
3. Season one side (the smooth side) of each chicken breast.
4. Place each chicken breast (smooth side down) in the air fryer basket. Season the other side.
5. Set the timer for 10 minutes.
6. After 10 minutes turn the chicken breasts over to allow them to cook on both sides.
7. Check the chicken is cooked all the way through - use a meat thermometer if necessary.
8. Leave the chicken to rest for 5 minutes before serving or slicing.
9. NOTE
10. Cooking Times
11. Cooking times will vary depending on your air fryer and the size of the chicken breasts. Use the following times as a guide:
12. 150g - 200g: 16 to 18 Mins.
13. 200g - 300g: 18 to 20 Mins.
14. Always check the chicken is cooked all the way through (the juices should run clear and there should be no pink bits).

Air Fryer Boneless Chicken Thighs Recipe

 Servings: 4-6   Cooking Time: 15 Mins.

Ingredients:

- 2 lbs boneless skinless chicken thighs
- 1 tsp. salt
- 1 tsp. paprika
- ½ tsp. White pepper
- 2 tsp. garlic powder
- 1 tsp. dry basil
- 1 tsp. oregano
- ½ tsp. pepper flakes
- 1 ½ tbsp. oil

Directions:

1. Marinade the chicken
2. Mix spice blend, pat chicken thighs dry with paper towel, then place chicken thighs in a bowl, add oil and seasoning blend.
3. Rub the seasoning in to ensure it's well blended into the chicken, cover with cling film and let it marinade for 30 mins to overnight in the refrigerator. If you are in a pinch with time, marinade for at least 10 mins
4. Air fry the chicken
5. After 10 mins, place marinated chicken thighs in the air fryer and air fry at 400°F / 200°C for 15 to 20 mins. Flipping halfway through. Chicken is cooked through when internal temperature reaches 165°F / 74°C
6. Let chicken rest for a minute before serving with your favorite side
7. NOTES
8. There is no need to spray the basket since the chicken marinade has oil. If you are concerned about sticking, use perforated parchment paper.
9. Do not overcrowd the basket. Cool in batches if needed.
10. The use of a meat thermometer is highly recommended when cooking meats. If you don't have one, check the meat for doneness by cutting it at the thickest part. It should be white and juice should run clear and not red.
11. This recipe was made in a non preheated air fryer. However if cooking in batches, subsequent batches may cook quicker since the air fryer got preheated during the first batch.

Air Fryer Turkey Legs

 Servings: 3-4   Cooking Time: 30 Mins.

Ingredients:

- 3 Turkey Legs
- 4 tbsp. butter or olive oil
- 1 tsp. paprika
- ½ tsp. salt
- ¼ tsp. garlic powder
- ¼ tsp. black pepper

Directions:

1. If using butter put it in a small microwave safe bowl melt microwave it until it is melted.

2. Add the seasonings to the melted butter or oil and stir to combine.

3. Pat the legs dry with a paper towel. Brush the seasoning mixture all over the drumsticks. Pull the skin back and brush a little bit underneath.

4. Use parchment paper in the bottom of the air fryer basket if desired to make cleanup easier.

5. Put the legs in the air fryer basket and air fry at 390 for 25-30 minutes.

6. The legs are done when they reach an internal temp of 165 degrees F. Always check the temperature with a meat thermometer, don't just go based on cooking time.

7. If the drumsticks need more cooking time return them to the air fryer for another 5-10 minutes additional time and check the internal temp again.

8. Let them rest for 5-10 minutes before serving.

9. NOTES

10. Suggested seasoning variations:

11. Cajun - 1 tsp. Cajun seasoning, 1/2 tsp. salt, 1/2 tsp. black pepper

12. Old Bay - 1 1/2 tsp. Old Bay, 1/2 tsp. garlic powder

13. Montreal - 2 tsp. Montreal spicy steak seasoning

14. Classic - 1 tsp. poultry seasoning, 1/2 tsp. salt, 1/2 tsp. black pepper

15. Reheat leftover drumsticks in the air fryer at 360 degrees F for about 10 minutes to warm them up.

Chicken Parmesan In The Air Fryer

 Servings: 4   Cooking Time: 10 Mins.

Ingredients:

- 2 8 oz. boneless skinless chicken breasts, sliced lengthwise to make 4 thinner cutlets
- 6 tsp. seasoned breadcrumbs, whole wheat or gluten-free
- 2 tsp. grated Parmesan cheese
- 1 tsp. butter, melted (or olive oil)
- 6 tsp. reduced fat mozzarella cheese, I used Polly-o
- 1/2 C. marinara
- olive oil spray

Directions:

1. Combine breadcrumbs and parmesan cheese in a bowl. Melt the butter in another bowl.

2. Lightly brush the butter onto the chicken, then dip into breadcrumb mixture.

3. When the air fryer is ready, transfer to the air fryer basket, in batches as needed and spray the top with oil.

4. Air fryer 360F° 5 minutes, turn and top each with 2 tsp. sauce and 1 1/2 tsp. of shredded mozzarella cheese.

5. Cook 3 more minutes or until cheese is melted.

Southern Fried Chicken

 Servings: 6   Cooking Time: 14 Mins.

Ingredients:

- Oil, for frying, preferably groundnut oil
- 3 eggs
- 240ml hot red pepper sauce
- 1 1/4kg chicken, cut into pieces
- 2 C. self-raising flour
- For the house seasoning
- 1 C. salt
- 1/4 C. pepper
- 1/4 C. garlic powder

Directions:

1. Heat the oil to 180C in a deep pan or fryer. Do not fill the pan more than half full with oil.

2. In a medium bowl, beat the eggs. Add enough hot sauce so the egg mixture is bright orange (about 240ml).

3. Season the chicken with the house seasoning. Dip the seasoned chicken in the egg and then coat well in the flour.

4. Place the chicken in the preheated oil and fry until brown and crisp. Cooking time is approximately 13-14 minutes for dark meat and 8-10 minutes for white meat.

5. House seasoning:

6. Mix the ingredients together and store in an air-tight container for up to 6 months.

Air Fryer Sesame Chicken Breast

 Servings: 2   Cooking Time: 30 Mins.

Ingredients:

- 2 chicken breasts (skin-on, boneless or bone-in)
- 2 tsp. sesame oil
- 1 tsp. kosher salt (plus more to taste)
- 1/2 tsp. black pepper
- 1 tsp. sweet paprika
- 1/4 tsp. cayenne pepper (optional)
- 1 tsp. granulated garlic (or garlic powder)
- 1 tsp. granulated onions (or onion powder)

Directions:

1. Rub the chicken breasts with sesame oil. Sprinkle salt, pepper and the rest of ingredients all over. Pat down and rub gently to ensure even coverage.

2. Place chicken breasts on the rack inside the air fryer, ensuring some space between the chicken breasts, skin side up.

3. Plug in your air fryer, set the temperature to 380F and the time to 20 minutes. When the 20 minutes of cooking is up, flip the breasts and continue cooking for another 10 minutes.

4. Remove chicken breasts from the air fryer and set on a plate. Let rest for 5 minutes, then serve.

Air Fryer Chicken Parmesan Meatballs

 Servings: 4   Cooking Time: 15 Mins.

Ingredients:

- 1 lb ground chicken breast
- 1 C. breadcrumbs
- 1 egg
- 1 tsp. Italian seasoning
- 1 tsp. ground black pepper
- 1/2 C. parmesan cheese
- 3/4 C. marinara sauce
- 1/2 C. shredded mozzarella cheese

Directions:

1. Mix the chicken, breadcrumbs, paremsan cheese, egg, and seasoning in a small mixing bowl.

2. Prepare the air fryer basket with a piece of parchment paper or nonstick cooking spray.

3. Roll the chicken mixture into nine 2" meatballs.

4. Place the meatballs onto the prepared Air Fryer basket in a single layer, leaving room in between the meatballs. (Do not preheat the air fryer for this recipe.)

5. Cook on 350 degrees Fahrenheit for 12 minutes, flipping the meatballs halfway through. Add marinara sauce on top of each chicken meatball and then top with mozzarella cheese. Cook on 350 for an additional 2 minutes.

6. Serve over noodles, in a hoagie bun, on sliders, or as an appetizer.

Air Fryer Frozen Chicken Wings

 Servings: 2　　 Cooking Time: 30 Mins.

Ingredients:

- 1 lb. (454 g) frozen chicken wings (Raw, Raw & Breaded, Pre-cooked – breaded &/or sauced)

Directions:

1. Place the frozen chicken wings in the air fryer basket and spread in an even layer (make sure they aren't overlapping). No oil spray is needed. See individual type below for cooking guidance.

2. FROZEN CHICKEN WINGS – RAW

3. Air Fry at 400°F/205°C for 18-30 minutes (depending on thickness), flipping the wings a couple times while cooking. Check for doneness & air fry longer if needed.

4. FROZEN CHICKEN WINGS – PRE-COOKED

5. Air Fry at 380°F/193°C for 18-30 minutes (depending on thickness), flipping the wings a couple times while cooking. Check for doneness & air fry longer if needed.

6. NOTES

7. Air Frying Tips and Notes:

8. No Oil Necessary. Cook Frozen – Do not thaw first.

9. Shake or turn if needed. Don't overcrowd the air fryer basket.

10. If cooking in multiple batches, the first batch will take longer to cook if Air Fryer is not already pre-heated. Recipe timing is based on a non-preheated air fryer.

11. Recipes were tested in 3.4 to 6 qt air fryers. If using a larger air fryer, the recipe might cook quicker so adjust cooking time.

12. Remember to set a timer to shake/flip/toss as directed in recipe.

How To Reheat Chicken In Air Fryer

 Servings: 4   Cooking Time: 8 Mins.

Ingredients:

- 8 Pieces Leftover fried chicken
- Oil spray
- Water or broth

Directions:

1. Place chicken in air fryer basket in a single layer. If reheating larger pieces spray some water or broth to keep them from drying out.
2. Set temperature to 360°F / 180°C and timer to 8 minutes. Hit the start button and begin reheating.
3. Flip the chicken half way through cooking time and start checking if it's fully warmed through at 6 minutes. The internal temperature should read 165°F / 74°C when warmed through.
4. Serve immediately.
5. NOTES
6. No need to preheat. This recipe was made in a non preheated air fryer. If you decide to, the chicken will cook at a shorter time than when the air fryer wasn't preheated. Please keep a close eye on it.
7. Try to cook similar sized chicken pieces so they cook evenly.
8. If reheating deep fried chicken you do not need to use oil however you may need it when reheating air fried chicken.
9. A little spritz of water may be needed when reheating larger pieces of chicken.

Air Fryer Roast Chicken

 Servings: X   Cooking Time: X Mins.

Ingredients:

- 4.25 lb. whole chicken

Directions:

1. Clean chicken and pat dry.
2. Sprinkle generously with dry rub or own seasonings.
3. Spray fry basket with cooking spray and place chicken into the basket with the legs facing down.
4. Roast chicken for 330 degrees Fahrenheit for 30 minutes.
5. Flip chicken.
6. Roast for 20 more minutes at 330 degrees Fahrenheit or until internal temperature of chicken is 165 degrees Fahrenheit.

Chicken Breast Air Fryer Recipe

 Servings: X   Cooking Time: X Mins.

Ingredients:

- Salt to add some taste
- Garlic powder
- A small amount of black pepper
- Melted butter

Directions:

1. Set your fryer to heat to about 400 degrees. Air fryers of different models have different temperature control settings. Consult your device manual to be sure.

2. Cut your chicken breasts into equal halves. Again the size to which you cut is determined by the capacity and size of your fryer.

3. Put the chicken in the fryer. Ensure the chicken stand against the sides of the air fryer basket.

4. Get some small bowl and mix all the spices and butter. Brush the mixture on the sides of the chicken.

5. Serve it while cool

6. Our Takeaways

7. Always ensure the chicken is placed in the fryer. It should stand against the sides of the air fryer basket. It helps to prevent the pieces of chicken from touching, making them cook evenly.

8. We do not recommend any air fryer preheating. You need to set up the temperature to the required level and start.

Healthy Air Fryer Herbed Chicken Breast

 Servings: 2   Cooking Time: 18 Mins.

Ingredients:

- 2 boneless, skinless chicken breasts (about 8 oz. (227g) each)
- oil spray or olive oil , to coat chicken
- 1/2 tsp. dried herb seasoning (basil, thyme, oregano, etc. - whatever you like best or any preferred seasoning)
- 1/2 tsp. salt , or to taste
- black pepper , to taste

Directions:

1. Pat dry the chicken breasts. For thicker chicken breasts, cut several 1/2" deep slits in the chicken so it will cook through to the middle better. Coat each chicken breast with oil, then season with dried herbs, salt, & pepper. Place the chicken in the air fryer basket or rack in a single layer.

2. Air Fry at 380°F(195°C) for 14-18 minutes, turning the chicken over halfway through cooking. Air fry the chicken until the internal temp is 165°F (75°C) in the thickest part. If you're cooking bone-in chicken breast, cook for additional 2-6 minutes, if needed.

3. Allow the chicken breast to rest for 5 minutes. Slice and serve while warm.

4. NOTES

5. Approximate Air Fryer Cooking Times for Different Sized Boneless Chicken Breasts cooked at 380°F/195°C: (for thicker chicken breasts, it is recommended to cut several 1/2" deep slits in the chicken so it will cook through to the middle better)

6. 6 oz. - 12-15 Mins.

7. 8 oz. - 14-18 Mins.

8. 10 oz. - 16-20 Mins.

9. 12-16 oz. - 18-22 Mins.

10. If cooking multiple chicken breasts, don't overcrowd the air fryer basket. Only cook in a single layer.

11. Recipe timing is based on a non-preheated air fryer. If air fryer is pre-heated, reduce cooking time by a few minutes.

12. Recipes were tested in 3.4 to 6 qt air fryers. If using a larger air fryer, the recipe might cook quicker so adjust cooking time.

13. Remember to set a timer to turn as directed in recipe.

How To Cook Frozen Chicken In The Air Fryer

 Servings: 5   Cooking Time: 26 Mins.

Ingredients:

- 5-8 Frozen, skinless raw chicken tenderloin
- Avocado oil
- Seasoning to taste. See BBQ chicken seasoning recipe suggestion.
- HOMEMADE BBQ CHICKEN SEASONING
- 1/4 C. chili powder
- 1 tbsp. paprika
- 1 tbsp. thyme
- 2 tsp. salt
- 2 tsp. garlic powder
- 1 tsp. black pepper
- 1 tsp. cumin
- 1 tsp. cayeene pepper
- 1 tbsp. brown sugar

Directions:

1. CHICKEN FROM FROZEN
2. Wash with water any ice off of the chicken and pat dry.
3. Lightly spray the chicken with avocado oil. Then season them to your taste.
4. Place the chicken in the air fryer basket (the amount of chicken you are able to cook depends on the size of your air fryer. Place them evenly spaced in the basket, making sure they don't overlap).
5. Cook at 360°F/180°C for 15 minutes, no need to preheat. After 15 minutes, flip the chicken and cook for an additional 8 minutes, or until the internal temperature reads 160-165°F/71.1-73.8°C.
6. Tent the chicken for 5-10 minutes, or until the chicken reaches safe temperature of 165°F/73.8°C.
7. HOMEMADE BBQ CHICKEN SEASONING
8. Combine ingredients together and mix well.
9. Store any leftover mix in an air tight container.

Air Fryer Turkey Avocado Burgers

 Servings: 4   Cooking Time: 15 Mins.

Ingredients:

- 1 lb. (454 g) ground turkey
- 2 cloves garlic , minced
- 1 tbsp. (15 ml) Worcestershire , fish sauce, or soy sauce (fish sauce is our favorite)
- 1 tsp. (5 ml) dried herbs (oregano, thyme, dill, basil, marjoram)
- 1/2 C. (80 g) minced fresh onion
- 1/2 tsp. (2.5 ml) salt , or to taste
- Lots of black pepper
- oil spray , for coating
- BURGER ASSEMBLY:
- 4 Buns
- 1 avocado , sliced
- Optional: cheese, radish sprouts, lettuce, tomato, etc.

Directions:

1. Preheat air fryer at 380°F/193°C for 5 minutes.

2. In bowl, combine turkey, garlic, Worcestershire sauce (or fish sauce or soy sauce), dried herbs, onion, salt and pepper. Mix everything until just combined.

3. Divide and flatten into 4 patties about 4" wide. Spray both sides with oil. If you have a smaller air fryer, you'll have to cook in two batches.

4. Air Fry at 380°F/193°C for 10-12 minutes, flip after 6 minutes. Cook to your preference or until the internal temperature reaches 165°F/74°C. If your patty is thicker, you many need to cook for a few more minutes.

5. For Turkey Cheeseburgers: add the slices of cheese on top of the cooked patties. Air fry at 380°F/193°C for about 30 seconds to 1 minute to melt the cheese.

6. For best juiciness, cover the patties and let rest for 3 minutes. Warm the buns in the air fryer at 380°F for about 1 minute while patties are resting. Serve on buns, topped with 1/4 avocado and your favorite burger toppings.

Pork, Beef & Lamb Recipes

Air-fryer Loaded Pork Burritos

 Servings: 6   Cooking Time: 10 Mins.

Ingredients:

- 3/4 C. thawed limeade concentrate
- 1 tbsp. olive oil
- 2 tsp. salt, divided
- 1-1/2 tsp. pepper, divided
- 1-1/2 lb. boneless pork loin, cut into thin strips
- 1 C. chopped seeded plum tomatoes
- 1 small green pepper, chopped
- 1 small onion, chopped
- 1/4 C. plus 1/3 C. minced fresh cilantro, divided
- 1 jalapeno pepper, seeded and chopped
- 1 tbsp. lime juice
- 1/4 tsp. garlic powder
- 1 C. uncooked long grain rice
- Cooking spray
- 3 C. shredded Monterey Jack cheese
- 6 flour tortillas (12 inches), warmed
- 1 can (15 ounces) black beans, rinsed and drained
- 1-1/2 C. sour cream

Directions:

1. In a large shallow dish, combine the limeade concentrate, oil, 1 tsp. salt and 1/2 tsp. pepper; add pork. Turn to coat; cover and refrigerate at least 20 minutes.

2. For salsa, in a small bowl, combine the tomatoes, green pepper, onion, 1/4 C. cilantro, jalapeno, lime juice, garlic powder, and remaining salt and pepper. Set aside.

3. Meanwhile, cook rice according to package directions. Stir in remaining cilantro; keep warm.

4. Drain pork, discarding marinade. Preheat air fryer to 350°. In batches, place pork in a single layer on greased tray in air-fryer basket; spritz with cooking spray. Cook until pork is no longer pink, 8-10 minutes, turning halfway through.

5. Sprinkle 1/3 C. cheese off-center on each tortilla. Layer each with 1/4 C. salsa, 1/2 C. rice mixture, 1/4 C. black beans and 1/4 C. sour cream; top with about 1/2 C. pork. Fold sides and ends over filling. Serve with remaining salsa.

Crispy Keto Parmesan Crusted Pork Chops In The Air Fryer

 Servings: 4   Cooking Time: 15 Mins.

Ingredients:

- 4 To 6 Thick Center Cut Boneless Pork Chops These Are My Favorite But You Can Use The Bone-In Pork Chops Also
- 1/2 tsp. Salt
- 1/4 tsp. Pepper
- 1 tsp. Smoked Paprika
- 1/2 tsp. Onion Powder
- 1/4 tsp. Chili Powder
- 2 Large Eggs Beaten
- 1 C. Pork Rind Crumbs
- 3 Tbs Grated Parmesan Cheese

Directions:

1. Preheat The Air Fryer To 400F For About 10 Minutes.
2. Season Both Sides Of Each Pork Chop With Salt And Pepper.
3. Use A Food Processor To Blend The Pork Rinds Into Crumbs.
4. Combine The Pork Rind Crumbs And Seasonings In A Large Bowl.
5. Place The Beaten Egg In A Separate Bowl.
6. Dip Each Pork Chop Into The Egg Mixture First, Then The Crumb Mixture Immediately After.
7. Place Each Pork Chop In The Basket.
8. Cook Them At 400 Degrees For 12 To 15 Minutes. 15 Minutes For The Really Thick Pork Chops. I Am Usually Able To Fit About 4 Or 5 Pork Chops In The Basket Of The Air Fryer At A Time.

Air Fryer Steak Bites And Mushrooms Recipe

 Servings: 4   Cooking Time: 10 Mins.

Ingredients:

- 1 lb. sirloin filet cut into 1 to 1-½ inch cubes
- 1 tbsp. olive oil
- 1 tbsp. Montreal seasoning
- 8 oz. mushrooms
- Easy Blue Cheese Sauce Optional

Directions:

1. Preheat empty air fryer with crisper plate or basket in place at 390°F for 3 minutes.

2. Pat meat dry.

3. While air fryer is heating up, toss beef cubes with olive oil and Montreal seasoning.

4. Chop mushrooms in half or in thirds.

5. Pour beef cubes and mushrooms into the preheated air fryer and gently shake to combine.

6. Set air fryer temperature to 390°F and timer for 7 minutes.

7. After 3 minutes pass, pause and shake the basket. Do this again at 2-minute intervals until the beef cubes reach the desired doneness. Mine finished in 7 minutes. The time will vary by machine and based upon the thickness of the cubes. The best way to determine if the meat is done is to pause and check it. Lift a large piece out and test it with a meat thermometer or cut and peek in the middle to see the progress. Note that the meat will continue to cook once it is removed from the air fryer and is resting. Meat is medium at 145°F and has a warm pink center.

8. Allow the meat to rest a couple of minutes before serving and then enjoy!

Air Fryer Cheese Stuffed Meatballs

 Servings: 3   Cooking Time: 13 Mins.

Ingredients:

- 4 oz. Burrata, cut into small cubes (or Mozzarella Cheese)
- 1 lb. Ground Beef (or ground meat of choice)
- 1 Egg
- 1 Jalapeno, Minced
- 1/4 C. Onion, finely chopped
- 4 Garlic Cloves, minced
- 1.5 tsp. Italian Seasoning
- 1 tsp. Paprika
- 1 tsp. Chili Powder
- 1/2 tsp. Garlic Powder
- 1/4 tsp. Black Pepper
- 1/2 tsp. Sea Salt
- 1/2 tsp. Red Crushed Peppers
- Marinara for serving

Directions:

1. Prepare the ground meat mixture by combining all the ingredients (except the cheese).

2. Preheat the air fryer to 370F for 5 minutes.

3. Scoop 3 tbsp. of the mixture and form into 2 small flat patties. Place a cube of cheese in the middle of one of the patties and use the other to place on top. Pinch meat up around cheese to seal and form into a ball. (You can also simply form a meatball, make a large indentation, place the cheese inside, and close the meatball.)

4. Place meatballs in the basket of the air fryer and cook at 370° for 13 minutes. Work in batches if needed to ensure the meatballs are not overcrowded in the air fryer.

5. Serve with warmed marinara and enjoy!

Airfryer Kofta Kabab Recipe Low Carb

 Servings: 4   Cooking Time: 10 Mins.

Ingredients:

- 1 tbsp. Oil
- 1 lb. Lean Ground Beef
- ¼ C. Chopped Parsley
- 1 tbsp. Minced Garlic
- 2 tbsp. kofta kabab spice mix
- 1 tsp. Kosher Salt

Directions:

1. Using a stand mixer, blend together all ingredients. If you have time, let the mixture sit in the fridge for 30 minutes. You can also mix it up and set aside for a day or two until you're ready to make the kababs

2. Although I tried this with and without skewers, it really makes no difference to the final product. Since it's a lot easier to simply shape the kababs by hand, divide the meat into four and make four long sausage shapes (or Pokémon shape or whatever you want).

3. Place the kababs in your airfryer and cook at 370F for 10 minutes.

4. Check with a meat thermometer to ensure that the kababs have an internal temperature of 145F.

5. Sprinkle with additional parsley for garnishing and serve with tzatziki, a cucumber tomato salad, and pita bread.

6. TO MAKE IN AN OVEN

7. Preheat the oven to 375F as you begin preparations.

8. Line a small baking pan with foil and then place a rack inside the pan. Your kababs should be placed on the rack so that the fat drips down.

9. You may choose to finish them off with a broil.

10. To make on the grill

11. Preheat grill to 375F as you begin preparations.

12. Mix together ingredients in a stand mixer

13. Place meat on skewers

14. Grill until kababs reach an internal temperature of 145F

15. I used 85% ground beef but you can use any kind of meat you'd like including ground chicken, ground lamb, or a combination of beef and lamb which would be fabulous.

16. If you use lean ground meat such as venison, or bison, or turkey, you may need to add a little more oil and/or cook until just done and be very careful to not overcook.

Easy Air Fried Meatballs Recipe

 Servings: 8   Cooking Time: X Mins.

Ingredients:

- 1 lb. ground beef
- 1 lb. mild Italian sausage
- ¼ C. onion, minced
- 2 cloves garlic, minced
- 2 tbsp. parsley, chopped
- 2 eggs

- 1½ C. parmesan cheese, grated
- salt and pepper
- ½ tsp. crushed red pepper flakes
- ½ tsp. Italian seasoning
- salt and pepper to taste

Directions:

1. Add beef, pork, onion, garlic, parsley, eggs and cheese to a large bowl.

2. Sprinkle meat mixture with a pinch of salt and pepper.

3. Mix with your hands until combined.

4. Form into 1 or 2 inch meatballs - this recipe will make about 25 meatballs.

5. Lightly spray sir fryer basket with olive oil cooking spray.

6. Add meatballs to air fryer basket, making sure they don't touch too much or over crowd the basket (work in batches if needed.)

7. Cook in air fryer for 13 minutes at 350 degrees, removing basket around 8 minutes to quickly rotate meatballs.

8. Meatballs should be 165 degrees internally when a thermometer is placed into the thickest part of the meatball.

Sweet And Savory Air Fryer Ham With Honey Brown Sugar Glaze

 Servings: 6   🕐 **Cooking Time: 35 Mins.**

Ingredients:

- 3-4 lb. ham pre-sliced, pre-cooked
- FOR GLAZE:
- 1/2 C. unsalted butter
- 1 C. brown sugar
- 1/2 C. honey
- 2 tbsp. Dijon mustard
- 1/4 tsp. cinnamon
- 1/4 tsp. ground cloves
- 4 cloves garlic minced

Directions:

1. Place 2 generous pieces of tinfoil in the air fryer.
2. Place pre sliced ham in the middle of the tinfoil and tightly close the tinfoil around the ham.
3. Warm the ham for 10 minutes at 350°F/175°C.
4. While the ham is warming, create the glaze. Brown the butter in a small saucepan over medium heat, until it begins to turn golden brown and aromatic. Swirl it around in the pan occasionally to help it brown evenly.
5. Stir in the brown sugar, honey, mustard, cinnamon, and cloves. Stir until sugar is dissolved, about 2 minutes.
6. Reduce heat to low and add the garlic. Cook for a minute or two until it becomes fragrant and just begins to simmer. Right as it begins to simmer, remove from heat and set aside. As it cools, it will become the consistency of a thick honey.
7. Once the ham is done warming, open the tinfoil and brush or spoon 1/3 of the glaze over the ham. Reclose the tinfoil and continue cooking in the air fryer for another 20 minutes at 350°F/175°C.
8. Open and fold down the tinfoil for this last cook time to create a slightly crispy outer layer. Brush or spoon another 1/3 of the glaze over the ham and cook in the air fryer for another 5 minutes at the same temperature, checking occasionally to prevent burning edges.
9. The last □ of the glaze can be used while serving the ham. It may need to be gently warmed for a few minutes again to thin out the glaze for serving since honey tends to thicken as it cools.

Cook Bbq Ribs

 Servings: X   Cooking Time: X Mins.

Ingredients:

- Little Kosher salt
- About 30 oz. of BBQ ribs. Do not bother about the type. Any can do.
- Poultry seasoning
- Around 3 lb. of fresh ribs.

Directions:

1. Some freshly grounded pepper. Again, this might not be necessary. Nevertheless, you can still consider it.

2. Lastly, ensure on your working table you have mustard powder and some brown sugar.

3. Preparation

4. The first thing to do is heating your air fryer to a high of 390 degrees.

5. Get a bowl and put it on the table. Inside the container, whisk together salt, sugar, garlic powder, onion powder, poultry seasoning, mustard powder, and pepper.

6. Coat the ribs by rubbing this mixture using your hands.

7. Get rid of the tissue using a paper towel.

8. To get the best results, ensure you arrange the ribs standing up in the air fryer bucket.

9. Cook them for about ten minutes, but flip them often to ensure proper cooking.

10. Conclusion

11. One thing to note, however, is that the time you take for cooking will mostly depend on the type of air fryer and the thickness of the ribs.

Perfect Air Fryer Steak

 Servings: 2   Cooking Time: 12 Mins.

Ingredients:

- 2 8 oz. Ribeye steak
- salt
- freshly cracked black pepper
- olive oil*
- Garlic Butter
- 1 stick unsalted butter softened
- 2 tbsp. fresh parsley chopped
- 2 tsp. garlic minced
- 1 tsp. Worcestershire Sauce
- 1/2 tsp. salt

Directions:

1. Garlic Butter

2. Prepare Garlic Butter by mixing butter, parsley garlic, worcestershire sauce, and salt until thoroughly combined.

3. Place in parchment paper and roll into a log. Refrigerate until ready to use.

4. Air Fryer Steak

5. Remove steak from fridge and allow to sit at room temperature for 20 minutes. Rub a little bit of olive oil on both side of the steak and season with salt and freshly cracked black pepper.

6. Grease your Air Fryer basket by rubbing a little bit of oil on the basket. Preheat Air Fryer to 400 degrees Fahrenheit. Once preheated, place steaks in air fryer and cook for 12 minutes, flipping halfway through.*

7. Remove from air fryer and allow to rest for 5 minutes. Top with garlic butter.

Gingery Pork Meatballs

 Servings: 4 Cooking Time: 30 Mins.

Ingredients:

- For noodles
- 6 oz. Rice noodles
- 1/2 c. Asian-style sesame dressing
- 1 large carrot, shaved with julienne peeler or cut into matchsticks
- 1/2 English cucumber, shaved with julienne peeler or cut into matchsticks
- 1 scallion, thinly sliced
- 1/4 c. Cilantro, chopped
- For meatballs
- 1 large egg
- 2 tsp. Grated lime zest plus 2 tsp. lime juice
- 1 1/2 tbsp. Honey
- 1 tsp. Fish sauce
- Kosher salt
- 1/2 c. Panko
- 1 cloves garlic, grated
- 2 scallions, finely chopped
- 1 tbsp. Grated fresh ginger
- 1 small jalapeño, seeds removed, finely chopped
- 1 lb. Ground pork
- 1/4 c. Cilantro, chopped

Directions:

1. Prepare noodles: Cook noodles per package directions. Rinse under cold water to cool, drain well and transfer to large bowl. Toss with dressing, carrot, cucumber and scallion; set aside.

2. Prepare meatballs: In large bowl, whisk together egg, lime zest and lime juice, honey, fish sauce and ½ tsp. salt; stir in panko and let sit 1 minute. Stir in garlic, scallions, ginger and jalapeño, then add pork and cilantro and mix to combine.

3. Shape into Tbsp-size balls and air-fry at 400°F (in batches, if necessary; balls can touch but should not be stacked), shaking basket occasionally, until browned and cooked through, 8 to 12 minutes. Fold cilantro into noodles and serve with meatballs.

Bacon Avocado Fries

 Servings: 24   Cooking Time: X Mins.

Ingredients:

- 3 avocados
- 24 thin strips of bacon
- 1/4 c. Ranch dressing, for serving

Directions:

1. Save to my recipes

2. For oven

3. Preheat oven to 425°. Slice each avocado into 8 equally-sized wedges. Wrap each wedge in bacon, cutting bacon if needed. Place on a baking sheet, seam side down.

4. Bake until bacon is cooked through and crispy, 12 to 15 minutes.

5. Serve with ranch dressing.

6. For air fryer

7. Slice each avocado into 8 equally-sized wedges. Wrap each wedge with a strip of bacon, cutting bacon if needed.

8. Working in batches, arrange in air fryer basket in a single layer. Cook at 400° for 8 minutes until bacon is cooked through and crispy.

9. Serve warm with ranch.

Easy 15-minute Air Fryer Pork Chops

 Servings: 4   Cooking Time: 10 Mins.

Ingredients:

- 4 boneless pork chops
- 2 tsp. oil
- 1 tbsp. Ranch seasoning mix
- salt and pepper
- chopped parsley

Directions:

1. Pat pork chops dry with a paper towel. Drizzle the oil over both sides of each pork chop, spread to coat evenly. Sprinkle dry Ranch seasoning mix evenly over both sides of each. Then season with salt and pepper.

2. Preheat air fryer to 380°F/193°C. Air fry pork for 10 minutes, flipping halfway, or until internal temperature of pork chops reaches 145°F/63°C. Cooking time may vary depending on thickness of the pork chops and your air fryer.

3. Garnish cooked pork chops with fresh chopped parsley, if desired.

Instant Pot Sloppy Joe

 Servings: 8   Cooking Time: 20 Mins.

Ingredients:

- 2 lb. (907 g) ground beef (preferrably a leaner meat)
- 1 tbsp. (15 ml) olive oil
- 1 (1) medium onion , diced
- 3-4 cloves (3 cloves) fresh garlic , minced
- 1 C. (240 g) Ketchup
- 1/2 C. (123 g) tomato sauce
- 2 tbsp. (30 ml) yellow mustard or dijon mustard
- 2 tbsp. (30 ml) Worcestershire sauce
- 1 tsp. (5 ml) chili powder
- Kosher salt , to taste
- black pepper , to taste
- FOR THE SANDWICH:
- 8 (8) burger buns , warmed or toasted
- 2 C. (226 g) shredded cheddar cheese , optional
- Pickles , optional

Directions:

1. FOR INSTANT POT

2. Turn Instant Pot on "Sauté". Add oil. Sauté onions and garlic until soft and fragrant. Add beef. Cook beef mixture for about 3 minutes, or until lightly browned.

3. Add ketchup, tomato sauce, mustard, Worcestershire sauce, chili powder, salt and pepper. Give the mixture a good stir.

4. Close the lid and pressure cook on high pressure for 10 minutes . (These are the steps we did for our Instant Pot: Close lid and close pressure release valve. Press "Cancel" to stop the "Sauté" setting. Press the "Manual" button. Set the time to 10 minutes.)

5. After the cooking time is complete, press "Cancel" and carefully release the pressure.

6. Serve the beef mixture between the bread and add your optional favorite toppings like cheese or pickles.

7. FOR SLOW COOKER

8. In slow cooker add all the sloppy joe ingredients except for the olive oil (ground beef, onion, garlic, ketchup, tomato sauce, mustard, worcestershire, salt and pepper). Gently mix together all the ingredients to make everything combine well.

9. Cover and cook the mixture on low for 7 hours or about 4 hours on high. After cooked, give the sloppy joe mixture a good stir. Serve the sloppy joe mixture between the bread and add your optional favorite toppings like cheese or pickles.

10. NOTES

11. Recipe was tested in a 4-quart slow cooker and a 6-quart Instant Pot.

Dash Air Fryer Burger Recipe

 Servings: 4 Cooking Time: 10 Mins.

Ingredients:

- 1 pound, 90% lean ground beef
- 1 beaten egg
- ½ tsp. garlic powder
- ¼ C. panko breadcrumbs
- ½ tsp. paprika, smoked
- 2 tsp. kosher salt
- ½ tsp. black pepper, ground
- ½ tsp. Worcestershire sauce
- ½ tsp. onion powder
- 1/8 tsp. cayenne pepper (optional)

Directions:

1. Mix all ingredients for burgers in a large bowl. Mix them thoroughly using your hand to fully blend.

2. Form the mixture into 4 to 5-inch patties, and put 2 patties at a time, into the Dash air fryer.

3. Set the temperature to 325°F and time to 10 Mins.

4. Check for the desired doneness after 10 minutes has lapsed, and remove from the air fryer when done.

5. Service along with your desired burger bun and other accompaniments.

Air Fryer Mozzarella-stuffed Meatballs

 Servings: 4 Cooking Time: 30 Mins.

Ingredients:

- 450 g beef mince
- 50 g bread crumbs
- 25 g freshly grated parmesan
- 5 g freshly chopped parsley
- 1 large egg
- 2 cloves garlic, crushed
- 1 tsp. Dried oregano
- Salt
- Freshly ground black pepper
- 85 g fresh mozzarella, cut into 16 cubes
- Marinara, for serving

Directions:

1. In a large bowl, combine beef, bread crumbs, parmesan, parsley, egg, garlic, and oregano. Season with salt and pepper.

2. Scoop about 2 tbsp. of meat and flatten into a patty in your hand. Place a cube of mozzarella in the centre and pinch meat up around cheese and roll into a ball. Repeat with remaining meat to make 16 total meatballs.

3. Working in batches as needed, place meatballs in basket of air fryer and cook at 190°c for 12 minutes.

4. Serve with warmed marinara.

Fish & Seafood Recipes

Paleo Air Fryer Salmon Cakes

 Servings: 4   Cooking Time: 15 Mins.

Ingredients:

- 1 lb. Fresh Atlantic Salmon Side (half a side)
- 1/4 C. Avocado, mashed
- 1/4 C. Cilantro, diced + additional for garnish
- 1 1/2 tsp. Yellow curry powder
- 1/2 tsp. Stonemill Sea Salt Grinder
- 1/4 C. + 4 tsp. Tapioca Starch, divided (40g) *Read notes for lower carb version
- 2 Organic Cage Free Brown Eggs
- 1/2 C. Organic Coconut Flakes (30g)
- Organic Coconut Oil, melted (for brushing)
- For the greens:
- 2 tsp. Organic Coconut Oil, melted
- 6 C. Organic Arugula & Spinach Mix, tightly packed
- Pinch of Stonemill Sea Salt Grinder

Directions:

1. Remove the skin from the salmon, dice the flesh, and add it into a large bowl.

2. Add in the avocado, cilantro, curry powder, sea salt and stir until well mixed. Then, stir in 4 tsp. of the tapioca starch until well incorporated.

3. Line a baking sheet with parchment paper. Form the salmon into 8, 1/4 cup-sized patties, just over 1/2 inch thick, and place them onto the pan. Freeze for 20 minutes so they are easier to work with.

4. While the patties freeze, pre-heat your Air Fryer to 400 degrees for 10 minutes, rubbing the basket with coconut oil. Additionally, whisk the eggs and place them into a shallow plate. Place the remaining 1/4 C. of Tapioca starch and the coconut flakes in separate shallow plates as well.

5. Once the patties have chilled, dip one into the tapioca starch, making sure it's fully covered. Then, dip it into the egg, covering it entirely, and gently brushing off any excess. Finally, press just the top and sides of the cake into the coconut flakes and place it, coconut flake-side up, into the air fryer. Repeat with all cakes.

6. Gently brush the tops with a little bit of melted coconut oil (optional, but recommended) and cook until the outside is golden brown and crispy, and the inside is juicy and tender, about 15 minutes. Note: the patties will stick to the Air Fryer basked a little, so use a sharp-edged spatula to remove them.

7. When the cakes have about 5 minutes left to cook, heat the coconut oil up in a large pan on medium heat. Add in the Arugula and Spinach Mix, and a pinch of salt, and cook, stirring constantly, until the greens JUST begin to wilt, only 30 seconds - 1 minute.

8. Divide the greens between 4 plates, followed by the salmon cakes. Garnish with extra cilantro and DEVOUR!

9. If you want to bake in the oven:

10. Preheat your oven to 400 degrees and line a baking sheet with parchment paper, placing a cooling rack

on top of the pan. Rub the cooling rack with coconut oil.

11. Place the patties, coconut-side up, onto the cooling rack and bake for 15-17 minutes until crispy. NOTE: we liked these better in the air fryer, as they do get a little crispier, but they are still good in the oven!

12. Notes

13. *To make these even lower carb:

14. Use 2 tsp. of coconut flour INSIDE the cakes, and then use the same 1/4 of coconut flour on the outside, before dipping in egg. This will save you about 4g of total carbs per serving, and will increase the fiber by about 4g per serving. We slightly prefer it with tapioca flour, as coconut does make them a little dryer, but its still super yummy!

15. **Depending on the size of your air fryer, you may need to cook these in two batches and keep the first batch warm in the oven.

Air Fryer Salmon Cakes

 Servings: 4 Cooking Time: 10 Mins.

Ingredients:

- 14.75 oz. salmon canned, deboned
- 2 eggs
- 1 tsp. mayonnaise
- 1/2 bell pepper red
- 1/2 C. breadcrumbs

- 1/2 tsp. garlic powder
- 1/2 tsp. black pepper
- 1/4 tsp. salt
- 2 tsp. fresh chopped parsley
- 1 tsp. olive oil spray

Directions:

1. Heat the air fryer to 390 degrees Fahrenheit. Prepare the Air Fryer basket.

2. Mix the salmon, breadcrumbs, eggs, and seasonings in a large bowl.

3. Measure out the salmon patties with ½ C. measuring cup.

4. Form the salmon cakes to be no larger than 1" thickness.

5. Add the salmon cakes to the prepared air fryer basket. Spray the tops of the patties and cook for 8 minutes.

6. Open the Air Fryer and flip the patties over, spray the top of the patties, and cook for an additional 2 minutes.

7. Serve with dill sauce or favorite dipping sauce.

Air Fryer Honey Mustard Salmon Recipe

 Servings: 3   Cooking Time: 10 Mins.

Ingredients:

- 3 salmon fillets 1 ½ inches thick
- salt and pepper
- 2 tbsp. honey
- 1 tbsp. Dijon mustard

Directions:

1. Make a foil sling for the air fryer basket, about 4 inches tall and a few inches longer than the width of the basket. Lay foil widthwise across basket, pressing it into and up the sides. Lightly spray foil and basket with cooking spray.

2. Pat salmon dry with paper towels. Season with salt and pepper.

3. In a small bowl, mix together honey and Dijon, until well combined. Reserve 1 tbsp. of glaze. Drizzle remaining glaze evenly over salmon fillets, tops and sides.

4. Arrange fillets skin side down on sling in the basket, with space between them. (The number of fillets you can fit in your air fryer at one time depends on the size of the fillets and the size of your air fryer.)

5. Cook at 350°F/175°C for 8-10 minutes, until salmon flakes easily and registers at 145°F/62.8°C (thinner salmon will be ready sooner, thicker salmon will take more time).

6. Using sling, carefully lift salmon from air fryer. Loosen the skin with a fish spatula or utensil, then transfer fillets to plate, leaving skin behind.

7. Drizzle reserved sauce over fillets. Garnish with fresh parsley, if desired. Serve warm.

8. NOTES

9. Works with skin-on fillets and fillets without skin.

Air Fryer Cajun Shrimp Dinner

 Servings: 4   Cooking Time: 20 Mins.

Ingredients:

- 1 tbsp. Cajun or Creole seasoning
- 24 (1 pound) cleaned and peeled extra jumbo shrimp
- 6 oz. fully cooked Turkey/Chicken Andouille sausage or kielbasa* (sliced)
- 1 medium zucchini (8 ounces, sliced into 1/4-inch thick half moons)
- 1 medium yellow squash (8 ounces, sliced into 1/4-inch thick half moons)
- 1 large red bell pepper (seeded and cut into thin 1-inch pieces)
- 1/4 tsp. kosher salt
- 2 tbsp. olive oil

Directions:

1. In a large bowl, combine the Cajun seasoning and shrimp, toss to coat.
2. Add the sausage, zucchini, squash, bell peppers, and salt and toss with the oil.
3. Preheat the air fryer 400F.
4. In 2 batches (for smaller baskets), transfer the shrimp and vegetables to the air fryer basket and cook 8 minutes, shaking the basket 2 to 3 times.
5. Set aside, repeat with remaining shrimp and veggies.
6. Once both batches are cooked, return the first batch to the air fryer and cook 1 minute.

Air Fryer Garlic Herb Salmon

 Servings: 2   Cooking Time: 10 Mins.

Ingredients:

- 2 salmon fillets (6 oz./170g each), skin and bones removed
- 1 tsp. dried herbs or 2 tsp. fresh chopped dill , thyme or oregano
- 1 tsp. garlic powder or 2 small cloves garlic,
minced
- salt , to taste
- black pepper , to taste
- olive oil or oil spray , for coating

Directions:

1. Prep the salmon: rinse and pat dry the salmon. Lightly coat with oil or oil spray. Season with herbs, garlic powder/minced garlic, salt and pepper.
2. Lay perforated silicone liner or perforated parchment paper inside basket or spray the bottom of basket. Place salmon in basket.
3. Air Fry at 380°F/193°C for about 6-10 minutes. Gently press the salmon to check its doneness (the firmer it is, the more fully cooked it is). Or check the salmon with a fork to make sure it's cooked to your preferred doneness.

Air Fryer Salmon, Potatoes, And Brussels Sprouts Bake Dinner Recipe

 Servings: 4   Cooking Time: X Mins.

Ingredients:

- 1/2 lb. red potatoes
- 1/2 lb. brussels sprouts
- 4 tbsp. avocado oil divided
- 5 tbsp. Maple Bacon Seasoning divided
- 2 8 oz. salmon fillets

Directions:

1. Prepare the Vegetables. Cut the red potatoes into bite sized pieces. Then, cut the brussels sprouts in half.

2. Combine the potatoes and brussels sprouts in a large bowl with 2½ tbsp. of avocado oil and 3½ tbsp. of Maple Bacon Seasoning. Mix together until everything is evenly coated.

3. Place brussel sprouts and potatoes in the air fryer basket and cook at 350°F/176°C for 5 minutes.

4. While the vegetables are cooking, take the salmon fillets and brush on both sides with the remaining 1½ tbsp. oil, and season with the remaining 1½ tbsp. Maple Bacon Seasoning.

5. Stir the vegetables in the air fryer basket. Add the salmon on top and cook for an additional 8-10 minutes at 350°F/176°C, or until the salmon reaches 145°F/62.7°C and flakes easily with a fork.

6. Remove the salmon from the air fryer basket. Test the brussel sprouts and potatoes with a fork. If done, remove from the air fryer basket and enjoy. If not, keep cooking in 1-2 minute increments until they reach desired tenderness.

Air Fryer Shrimp

 Servings: 4　　 Cooking Time: 5 Mins.

Ingredients:

- 1 lb. large shrimp raw; remove shell and tail if desired; note 1
- 1 1/2 tbsp. olive oil
- 1 1/2 tbsp. lime juice note 2
- 1 1/2 tbsp. honey note 3
- 2 cloves garlic minced
- 1/8 tsp. salt

Directions:

1. Marinade - In a large bowl, stir together the olive oil, lime juice, honey, garlic and salt. Add the shrimp and marinate for 20-30 minutes.

2. Cook - Heat the air fryer to 390°F/200°C.Shake excess marinade off the shrimp and put the whole batch in the air fryer.

3. Cook for 2 minutes, give the basket a good shake, and return to the air fryer. Cook for another 2-3 minutes, or until shrimp are pink and cooked through.

4. Serve - with lime wedges and cilantro.

Air Fryer 3 Ingredient Fried Catfish

 Servings: 4　　 Cooking Time: 20 Mins.

Ingredients:

- 4 catfish fillets
- 1/4 C. Louisiana Fish Fry Coating
- 1 tsp. olive oil
- 1 tsp. chopped parsley optional

Directions:

1. Pat the catfish dry.

2. Sprinkle the fish fry onto both sides of each fillet. Ensure the entire filet is coated with seasoning.

3. Spritz olive oil on the top of each filet.

4. Place the filet in the Air Fryer basket. Do not stack the fish and do not overcrowd the basket. Cook in batches if needed. Close and cook for 10 minutes on 400 degrees.

5. Open the air fryer and flip the fish. Cook for an additional 10 minutes.

6. Open and flip the fish.

7. Cook for an additional 2-3 minutes or until desired crispness.

8. Top with optional parsley.

Gowise Air Fryer Chipotle Tuna Melt Recipe

 Servings: 2   Cooking Time: 8 Mins.

Ingredients:

- 2 slices Italian bread
- 2 Chipotle pepper in adobo sauce
- ½ C. mayonnaise
- 12 oz. Tuna
- 1 slice American cheese
- Pinch of cilantro
- Pinch of black pepper
- Butter
- Pinch of garlic salt

Directions:

1. Blend Chipotle peppers in mayonnaise. Then, combine with black pepper and garlic salt.

2. Transfer the mixture into a medium-size bowl. Toss in the tuna and stir to blend well. Add cilantro, pepper or salt to give taste.

3. Smear the toast liberally with butter. Then, spread the tuna onto the buttered slice of bread and top with cheese and bread. Spread butter over the top slice.

4. Lay the sandwich on the Gowise air fryer basket and cook at 320 degrees Fahrenheit for about 4 minutes.

5. Take the cooked sandwich out of the fryer basket as soon as the cheese has melted or when toast turns golden.

6. Serve immediately for 1 adult or 2 kids.

Air Fryer Salmon

 Servings: 2   Cooking Time: 10 Mins.

Ingredients:

- 2 (170g) salmon fillets
- Salt
- Freshly ground black pepper
- 2 tsp. Extra-virgin olive oil
- 2 tbsp. Whole grain mustard
- 1 tbsp. Packed brown sugar
- 1 clove garlic, crushed
- 1/2 tsp. Thyme leaves

Directions:

1. Season salmon all over with salt and pepper. In a small bowl, whisk together oil, mustard, sugar, garlic, and thyme. Spread on top of salmon.

2. Arrange salmon in air fryer basket. Set air fryer to 200°c and cook for 10 minutes.

Air Fryer Shrimp Cocktail

 Servings: 6   Cooking Time: 10 Mins.

Ingredients:

- FOR THE SHRIMP
- 1 lb. (455 g) raw shrimp , deveined and shells removed
- 1 tsp. (5 ml) oil , to coat shrimp
- salt , to taste
- black pepper , to taste
- SHRIMP COCKTAIL SAUCE
- 1/2 C. (120 g) ketchup (or low-carb tomato sauce for keto)
- 2 tsp. (10 ml) Worcestershire sauce
- 1 tsp. (5 ml) prepared horseradish
- 1 tsp. (5 ml) fresh lemon juice
- 1/4 tsp. (1.25 ml) celery salt
- 1/4 tsp. (1.25 ml) garlic powder
- 1/4 tsp. (1.25 ml) salt , or to taste
- black pepper to taste
- fresh lemon slices
- 1 (1) small cucumber , sliced (optional)
- fresh herbs for garnish (optional)

Directions:

1. In bowl, combine ketchup, Worcestershire sauce, horseradish, fresh lemon juice, celery salt, garlic powder, salt and black pepper. Stir until well mixed then set aside.

2. After shrimp shells are removed and de-veined, rinse and pat dry the shrimp. Coat shrimp with oil, and then season with salt and pepper. Place the shrimp in the air fryer basket or tray in a single layer.

3. Air Fry shrimp at 400°F for 8-12 minutes, or until cooked through. Shrimp comes in different sizes so check halfway through to make sure it's cooked enough or to your liking. After air frying, let the shrimp cool completely and chill in the fridge until ready to serve.

4. Serve the cooked shrimp with the shrimp cocktail sauce and slices of fresh lemon and cucumbers. Garnish with fresh herbs if you are feeling fancy.

Air-fryer Fish And Fries

 Servings: 4   Cooking Time: 25 Mins.

Ingredients:

- 1 lb. potatoes (about 2 medium)
- 2 tbsp. olive oil
- 1/4 tsp. pepper
- 1/4 tsp. salt
- fish:
- 1/3 C. all-purpose flour
- 1/4 tsp. pepper
- 1 large egg
- 2 tbsp. water
- 2/3 C. crushed cornflakes
- 1 tbsp. grated Parmesan cheese
- 1/8 tsp. cayenne pepper
- 1 lb. haddock or cod fillets
- 1/4 tsp. salt
- Tartar sauce, optional

Directions:

1. Preheat air fryer to 400°. Peel and cut potatoes lengthwise into 1/2-in.-thick slices; cut slices into 1/2-in.-thick sticks.

2. In a large bowl, toss potatoes with oil, pepper and salt. Working in batches, place potatoes in a single layer on tray in air-fryer basket; cook until just tender, 5-10 minutes Toss potatoes to redistribute; cook until lightly browned and crisp, 5-10 minutes longer.

3. Meanwhile, in a shallow bowl, mix flour and pepper. In another shallow bowl, whisk egg with water. In a third bowl, toss cornflakes with cheese and cayenne. Sprinkle fish with salt. Dip into flour mixture to coat both sides; shake off excess. Dip in egg mixture, then in cornflake mixture, patting to help coating adhere.

4. Remove fries from basket; keep warm. Place fish in a single layer on tray in air-fryer basket. Cook until fish is lightly browned and just beginning to flake easily with a fork, 8-10 minutes, turning halfway through cooking. Do not overcook. Return fries to basket to heat through. Serve immediately. If desired, serve with tartar sauce.

Popcorn Shrimp Tacos With Cabbage Slaw

 Servings: 4   Cooking Time: X Mins.

Ingredients:

- 2 C. coleslaw mix
- 1/4 C. minced fresh cilantro
- 2 tbsp. lime juice
- 2 tbsp. honey
- 1/4 tsp. salt
- 1 jalapeno pepper, seeded and minced, optional
- 2 large eggs
- 2 tbsp. 2% milk
- 1/2 C. all-purpose flour
- 1-1/2 C. panko bread crumbs
- 1 tbsp. ground cumin
- 1 tbsp. garlic powder
- 1 lb. uncooked shrimp (41-50 per pound), peeled and deveined
- Cooking spray
- 8 corn tortillas (6 inches), warmed
- 1 medium ripe avocado, peeled and sliced

Directions:

1. In a small bowl, combine coleslaw mix, cilantro, lime juice, honey, salt and, if desired, jalapeno; toss to coat. Set aside.

2. Preheat air fryer to 375°. In a shallow bowl, whisk eggs and milk. Place flour in a separate shallow bowl. In a third shallow bowl, mix panko, cumin and garlic powder. Dip shrimp in flour to coat both sides; shake off excess. Dip in egg mixture, then in panko mixture, patting to help coating adhere.

3. In batches, arrange shrimp in a single layer on greased tray in air-fryer basket; spritz with cooking spray. Cook until golden brown, 2-3 minutes. Turn; spritz with cooking spray. Cook until golden brown and shrimp turn pink, 2-3 minutes longer.

4. Serve shrimp in tortillas with coleslaw mix and avocado.

Quick And Healthy Tilapia In The Air Fryer

 Servings: 2   Cooking Time: 8 Mins.

Ingredients:

- 1 lb. tilapia
- 2 eggs
- 1 package Louisiana fish fry

Directions:

1. Preheat the air fryer to 400°F/200°C for 5 minutes.
2. Wash the tilapia and pat it dry.
3. In a shallow bowl, whisk the eggs.
4. In a separate shallow bowl or plate, pour out the package of the Louisiana fish fry.
5. Place the tilapia in the egg wash. Be sure to cover both sides.
6. Then, place the tilapia in the fish fry, once again covering both sides with it.
7. Spray the air fryer basket with oil. Place the fish in the air fryer basket. Spray with oil and cook at 350°F/177°C for 8 minutes.
8. With an instant read thermometer, make sure the fish registers at 145°F/63°C before consuming.
9. Enjoy with a dipping sauce of your choice! I loved serving it with a sweet garlic chili sauce.

Air-fryer Crumb-topped Sole

 Servings: 4   Cooking Time: 10 Mins.

Ingredients:

- 3 tbsp. reduced-fat mayonnaise
- 3 tbsp. grated Parmesan cheese, divided
- 2 tsp. mustard seed
- 1/4 tsp. pepper
- 4 sole fillets (6 oz. each)
- 1 C. soft bread crumbs
- 1 green onion, finely chopped
- 1/2 tsp. ground mustard
- 2 tsp. butter, melted
- Cooking spray

Directions:

1. Preheat air fryer to 375°. Combine mayonnaise, 2 tbsp. cheese, mustard seed and pepper; spread over tops of fillets.
2. In batches, place fish in a single layer on greased tray in air-fryer basket. Cook until fish flakes easily with a fork, 3-5 minutes.
3. Meanwhile, in a small bowl, combine bread crumbs, onion, ground mustard and remaining 1 tbsp. cheese; stir in butter. Spoon over fillets, patting gently to adhere; spritz topping with cooking spray. Cook until golden brown, 2-3 minutes longer. If desired, sprinkle with additional green onions.

Sweets & Desserts Recipes

Air Fryer,herb Butter Dinner Rolls

 Servings: 8   Cooking Time: 5 Mins.

Ingredients:

- 8 rolls frozen
- 1/4 C. butter melted, unsalted
- 2 tablspoons Italian seasoning

Directions:

1. Spread the frozen rolls onto the baking sheet or in the air fryer basket.
2. In a small bowl, mix the melted butter with the herbs.
3. Brush on the butter and herb mixture onto the rolls.
4. Set in the air fryer at 320 degrees F, for 5 minutes.
5. Plate, serve and enjoy!

Air Fryer Beignet Recipe

 Servings: 9   Cooking Time: 6 Mins.

Ingredients:

- 3 C. flour
- 1 C. milk
- 2 tsp. butter
- 2 tsp. brown sugar
- 1 pack active dry yeast
- 1 medium egg
- 1 1/2 tsp. salt
- 1 tsp. vanilla extract
- 1 sprinkle powdered sugar to taste

Directions:

1. Mix flour, salt, and instant yeast together in a small bowl.
2. Heat the milk in microwave until boiling hot.
3. Combine butter and sugar in a mixing bowl and pour the steaming milk over the top. Stir so that the butter melts and the sugar dissolves. Allow to cool to a lukewarm temp.
4. Add the egg and vanilla to the milk mixture and mix thoroughly.
5. Add the wet ingredients to the dry ingredients and mix until a dough is formed. Knead dough for 3-5 minutes.
6. Place dough into a lightly oiled bowl. Cover and allow it to rise for about 1 hour or until it has doubled in size.
7. Roll out dough to about 1/4 inch thick on a floured surface and cut into squares.
8. Set dough pieces aside for 30 minutes or until they have almost doubled in size.
9. Set airfryer at 390 degrees and cook dough squares for 6 minutes, flipping them over halfway through.
10. Cover with powdered sugar and enjoy!

Air Fryer Pumpkin Seeds Recipe

 Servings: 4   Cooking Time: 10-15 Mins.

Ingredients:

- 1 (10- to 15-pound) large pumpkin
- 1 tsp. olive oil
- 1/4 tsp. ground chipotle pepper
- 1/4 tsp. kosher salt, plus more as needed
- 1/8 tsp. cayenne pepper

Directions:

1. Cut the top off a large pumpkin and scoop out the seeds. Rinse in a colander under running water to separate from the pulp. Lay the seeds out on paper towels and pat dry. Let sit for 30 minutes to remove any excess moisture. You should have about 1 C. pumpkin seeds.
2. Heat the air fryer to 350°F. Transfer the dried pumpkin seeds to a medium bowl. Add 1 tsp. olive oil, 1/4 tsp. ground chipotle pepper, 1/4 tsp. kosher salt, and 1/8 tsp. cayenne pepper. Toss to combine.
3. Spread the seeds evenly in the basket of the air fryer. Cook, shaking the basket halfway through cooking, until the seeds are golden and crispy, 10 to 15 minutes total. Transfer to a bowl and let cool. Taste and season with more salt as needed.

Chocolate And Chilli Brownies In The Air Fryer

 Servings: X   Cooking Time: X Mins.

Ingredients:

- 200 g butter, melted
- 100 g cocoa powder
- 75 g dark chocolate, melted
- 2 large eggs
- 150 g caster sugar
- 1/2 tsp. vanilla essence
- 150 g self-raising flour
- 1 level tsp. crushed dried chilli flakes

Directions:

1. Preheat airfryer to 180C/350F
2. Mix butter, sugar and crushed dried chillies.
3. Beat the eggs and mix them in. Add the melted chocolate and vanilla extract.
4. Slowly add in the flour and cocoa powder. Mix gently, do not over stir.
5. Using a greased, or baking paper lined tin/container, pour the mixture in.
6. Cook in the air fryer for 15 to 20 minutes, checking a few times to make sure the top isn't burning - if it is cooking quickly, put some foil or baking paper on top.
7. Once ready, allow to cool and then cut into smaller portions to serve.

Air-fryer Acorn Squash Slices

 Servings: 6   Cooking Time: 15 Mins.

Ingredients:

- 2 medium acorn squash
- 2/3 C. packed brown sugar
- 1/2 C. butter, softened

Directions:

1. Preheat air fryer to 350°. Cut squash in half lengthwise; remove and discard seeds. Cut each half crosswise into 1/2-in. Slices; discard ends. In batches, arrange squash in a single layer on greased tray in air-fryer basket. Cook until just tender, 5 minutes per side.

2. Combine sugar and butter; spread over squash. Cook 3 minutes longer.

Air-fryer Wasabi Crab Cakes

 Servings: 2   Cooking Time: 10 Mins.

Ingredients:

- 1 medium sweet red pepper, finely chopped
- 1 celery rib, finely chopped
- 3 green onions, finely chopped
- 2 large egg whites
- 3 tbsp. reduced-fat mayonnaise
- 1/4 tsp. prepared wasabi
- 1/4 tsp. salt
- 1/3 C. plus 1/2 C. dry bread crumbs, divided
- 1-1/2 C. lump crabmeat, drained
- Cooking spray
- SAUCE:
- 1 celery rib, chopped
- 1/3 C. reduced-fat mayonnaise
- 1 green onion, chopped
- 1 tbsp. sweet pickle relish
- 1/2 tsp. prepared wasabi
- 1/4 tsp. celery salt

Directions:

1. Preheat air fryer to 375°. Combine first 7 ingredients; add 1/3 C. bread crumbs. Gently fold in crab.

2. Place remaining bread crumbs in a shallow bowl. Drop heaping tbsp. crab mixture into crumbs. Gently coat and shape into 3/4-in.-thick patties. In batches, place patties in a single layer on greased tray in air-fryer basket. Spritz crab cakes with cooking spray. Cook until golden brown, 8-12 minutes, carefully turning halfway through cooking and spritzing with additional cooking spray.

3. Meanwhile, place sauce ingredients in food processor; pulse 2 or 3 times to blend or until desired consistency is reached. Serve crab cakes immediately with dipping sauce.

Air Fryer Bacon Ritz Crackers Appetizer Recipe

 Servings: 8   Cooking Time: 6 Mins.

Ingredients:

- 1 Sleeve Ritz crackers
- ½ lb. bacon (about 8 slices of Thin sliced bacon)
- 4 tbsp. brown sugar

Directions:

1. Cut each bacon into 4 parts
2. Place bacon on each piece of crackers add ¼ to ½ tsp. of brown sugar over the bacon on each cracker. Ligtly press brown sugar down on the bacon.
3. Transfer crackers to the air fryer basket, set temperature to 400°F / 200°C and air fry for 5 to 6 mins.
4. NOTES
5. The caramelized sugar would be hot, so be careful when getting it out. It's best to let it cool slightly before trying to get it out.
6. When the crackers are hot, they would be soft. Don't worry, they crisp up as they cool.
7. Bacon wrapped crackers will take an extra minute to cook.

Coca Cola Funnel Cake

 Servings: 6   Cooking Time: 15 Mins.

Ingredients:

- 240g flour
- 1 tsp. baking powder
- 2 eggs, lightly beaten
- 355ml Coca-Cola
- Oil (for deep frying)
- 235ml Coca-Cola syrup
- Whipped cream
- Maraschino cherry

Directions:

1. In a medium bowl, mix together the flour and baking powder.
2. Mix in eggs and Coca Cola and stir until a smooth batter forms.
3. Preheat oil in a skillet or deep fryer.
4. Pour 1/3 C. of batter into a funnel or turkey baster and in a circular motion pour batter into the hot oil.
5. Fry up for about a minute on each side and drain on paper towels.
6. Serve while still warm and top with Coca Cola syrup, whipped cream and a maraschino cherry.

Air Fryer Churro Bites With Chocolate Dipping Sauce

 Servings: 24   Cooking Time: X Mins.

Ingredients:

- 1 C. water
- 8 tbsp. (1 stick) unsalted butter, cut into 8 pieces
- 1/2 C. plus 1 tbsp. granulated sugar, divided
- 1 C. all-purpose flour
- 1 tsp. vanilla extract
- 3 large eggs
- 2 tsp. ground cinnamon
- 4 oz. finely chopped dark chocolate
- 1/4 C. sour cream or Greek yogurt

Directions:

1. Bring the water, butter, and 1 tbsp. of the sugar to a simmer in a small saucepan over medium-high heat. Add the flour and quickly stir it in with a sturdy wooden spoon. Continue to cook, stirring constantly, until the flour smells toasted and the mixture is thick, about 3 minutes. Transfer to a large bowl.

2. Using the same wooden spoon, beat the flour mixture until cooled slightly but still warm, about 1 minute of constant stirring. Stir in the vanilla. Stir in the eggs one at a time, making sure each egg is incorporated before adding the next.

3. Transfer the dough to a piping bag or gallon zip-top bag. Let the dough rest for 1 hour at room temperature. Meanwhile, prepare the cinnamon sugar and chocolate sauce.

4. Combine the cinnamon and remaining 1/2 C. sugar in large bowl. Microwave the chocolate in a medium microwave-safe mixing bowl in 30-second intervals, stirring between each, until the chocolate is melted, 1 1/2 to 2 minutes. Add the sour cream or yogurt and whisk until smooth. Cover and set aside.

5. Preheat the air fryer for 10 minutes at 375°F. Pipe the batter directly into the preheated air fryer, making 6 (3-inch) pieces and piping them at least 1/2-inch apart. Air fry until golden-brown, about 10 minutes. Immediately transfer the churros to the bowl of cinnamon sugar and toss to coat. Repeat with air frying the remaining batter. Serve the churros warm with the dipping sauce.

Canned Refrigerated Biscuits In Air Fryer

 Servings: 8   Cooking Time: 10 Mins.

Ingredients:

- 1 can refrigerated biscuits
- oil spray

Directions:

1. Spray the air fryer basket or racks with oil to keep the biscuits from sticking. We don't suggest using parchment paper underneath because you want maximum air flow under the biscuits to help them cook all the way though. The parchment paper prevents maximum air flow under the biscuits.
2. Lay biscuits in single layer of air fryer basket or racks. Make sure to space them out so they aren't touching & have room to rise & expand.
3. For Grand Or Large Biscuits (Homemade Buttermilk Style And Flaky Layers Style):
4. Air Fry at 330°F/165°C for about 6-7 minutes. Gently wiggle the biscuits to loosen from the baskets.
5. Continue to Air Fry for another 1-3 minutes, or until they are crispy brown and cooked through.
6. You can also flip the biscuits to finish off during the last 1-3 minutes of air frying (they won't be as pretty, but is neccesary in some air fryers).
7. For Smaller Size Biscuits (Homemade Buttermilk Style And Flaky Layers Style):
8. Air Fry at 330°F/165°C for 5 minutes. Flip the biscuits and air fry for another 2-4 minutes, or until they are crispy brown and cooked through.

Easy Air Fryer Donuts

 Servings: 8   Cooking Time: 6 Mins.

Ingredients:

- Air Fryer Donuts
- 1 can store-bought flaky biscuit dough refrigerated
- 1 tsp. coconut oil spray
- Cinnamon Sugar
- 2 tsp. cinnamon
- 1/2 C. sugar
- 3 tsp. unsalted butter melted
- Glazed
- 1 C. powdered sugar
- 3 tsp. milk
- 1 tsp. vanilla extract

Directions:

1. Air Fryer Donuts
2. Remove the biscuit dough from the can and place it on a cutting board. Slice the dough into eight equal pieces. Using a rolling pin, flatten each piece of dough.
3. Cut a hole in a center of each dough circle.
4. Spray the air fryer basket with oil. Air fry donuts at 350°F for 2-3 minutes on each side or until they turn golden brown.
5. Cinnamon Sugar
6. In a shallow bowl, combine the cinnamon and sugar. Stir and set aside.
7. Brush each donut with melted butter. Dip each donut into the cinnamon-sugar mixture until coated. Enjoy!
8. Glaze
9. In a shallow bowl, combine the powdered sugar, milk, and vanilla extract. Whisk until the glaze is perfectly smooth.
10. Coat each donut with the glaze. Optional: Top with sprinkles.

Air Fryer Donuts + Donut Holes With A Sweet Glaze

 Servings: 12   Cooking Time: 16 Mins.

Ingredients:

- 1 C. milk warmed to about 110°F/43°C (240 grams)
- 2 ½ tsp. active dry yeast or instant yeast 7.75 grams
- ¼ C. sugar plus 1 tsp. (54 grams)
- ½ tsp. kosher salt 3 grams
- 1 large egg
- 4 tbsp. unsalted butter 57 grams

- 3 C. all-purpose flour 384 grams
- Oil spray
- GLAZE:
- 6 tbsp. unsalted butter 85 grams
- 2 C. powdered sugar 224 grams
- 2 tsp. vanilla extract 8 grams
- 2 to 4 tbsp. hot water 29-58 grams

Directions:

1. In a large bowl or bowl of a stand mixer (fitted with dough hook), combine the warm milk, 1 tsp. sugar, and the yeast. Let sit for about 5-10 minutes, until foamy.

2. Meanwhile, melt the butter and lightly beat the egg.

3. Add remaining ¼ C. sugar, salt, and egg to the yeast mixture; stir or whisk to combine. Then mix in the melted butter and 2 C. of flour on low speed.

4. Scrape down the sides of bowl, then mix in remaining 1 C. flour. Dough should start to pull away from sides of bowl, but still be sticky. (Can add up to ¼ C. flour more, if needed.) Increase speed to medium-low and knead for 5 minutes. Dough will become more smooth and elastic, but still sticky.

5. Remove dough hook or transfer dough to a greased bowl, cover with plastic wrap and let rise until doubled. (With instant yeast, this will probably take about 30 minutes.)

6. Punch down dough and turn out on lightly floured surface. Gently roll out dough until a little less than ½-inch thick, between ¼-inch and ½-inch. Cut out as many donuts as you can with a round cutter, about 3 inches in diameter. Use a cutter about 1 inch in diameter to cut out the centers.

7. Transfer cut out dough to a lightly greased parchment paper or silicone mat. Cover loosely with greased plastic wrap. Let rise until doubled, about 20-30 minutes.

8. Preheat air fryer to 350°F/177°C. Lightly spray air fryer basket with oil spray. Carefully transfer donuts to basket in a single layer. Lightly spray donuts with oil spray and cook until lightly golden brown, about 4 minutes. Cooking time will vary depending on your air fryer and the thickness of your donuts, so keep an eye on it! Repeat with remaining donuts, then with the donut holes. Transfer donuts to a cooling rack.

9. Glaze: While donuts are in the air fryer, melt butter for the glaze in a medium bowl or saucepan. Stir or

whisk in the powdered sugar and vanilla, until smooth. Stir or whisk in the hot water 1 tbsp. at a time until it reaches desired consistency, somewhat thin but not watery.

10. While donuts are still warm, but after cooling for a few minutes, submerge each into the glaze. For donut holes, glaze last and just dump them into the bowl and gently stir to coat.

11. Move cooling rack over the parchment paper used earlier or a piece of foil to make cleanup easier. Place the glazed donuts on the rack to allow excess to drip off and let sit until glaze hardens, about 10 minutes.

Air Fryer Mug Cake

 Servings: 2   Cooking Time: 12 Mins.

Ingredients:

- Kitchen Gadgets:
- Air Fryer
- Mug Cake Ingredients:
- 100 g Squares of Chocolate
- 100 g Squares of Chocolate broken
- 1 tsp. Butter heaped
- 1 tsp. Honey
- 1 tsp. Greek Yoghurt
- 1 tsp. Self Raising Flour
- 1 tsp. Vanilla Essence optional
- 1 tsp. Cocoa Powder optional

Directions:

1. Into two ramekins add squares of chocolate along with your butter and honey.
2. Place in the air fryer and cook for 2 minutes at 120c/250f to melt the chocolate.
3. Stir and add in Greek yoghurt. It will now be lovely and creamy. Then add in your second lot of chocolate which will be crushed. Stir well.
4. Add in self raising flour and cocoa powder or vanilla if you are using it. Stir well.
5. Cook for 10 minutes at 180c/360f and enjoy!

Air Fryer Banana Bread

 Servings: 1 Cooking Time: 30 Mins.

Ingredients:

- 2 ripe bananas, medium in size
- 120g butter, softened
- 100g caster sugar
- 200g self-raising flour
- 2 medium eggs, beaten
- 1tsp baking powder
- 1tsp ground cinnamon

Directions:

1. Mix together the butter and sugar until they are smooth. Then slowly add the beaten eggs and mix until they are combined.

2. Add the flour, baking powder and ground cinnamon, followed by the mashed bananas.

3. Stir everything together gently until combined.

4. Transfer the mixture to a greased baking tin and place it in the air fryer at 160°C. Set the timer for 30 minutes.

5. At the end of the cooking time, the banana bread should be browned on the outside and cooked all the way through. Insert a metal skewer to check it isn't wet or soggy on the inside. If it needs to be cooked for longer, check on it every 5 minutes to ensure it doesn't burn. If the outside is already browned, you might need to cover it in some foil.

Frozen Peaches

 Servings: 4 Cooking Time: X Mins.

Ingredients:

- 4 oz. granulated sugar
- 1 tsp. ground children's Vitamin C
- 1/2 tsp. smoked paprika
- 1 lb. peeled and pitted fresh peaches, cut into 1/2-inch thick slices

Directions:

1. Place the sugar, Vitamin C and paprika into a 1-gallon zip-top bag, seal and shake to combine. Add the peaches and toss to coat well. Lay the bag flat on a counter and using a straw, suck out any remaining air in the bag. Return to the freezer.

Snacks & Side Dishes Recipes

Air Fryer Sweet Potato Wedges

 Servings: 4   Cooking Time: 20 Mins.

Ingredients:

- 4 large sweet potatoes*
- 1 tsp. oil (I used olive oil)
- 1 tsp. smoked paprika
- 1 tsp. garlic powder
- Salt and pepper according to taste

Directions:

1. Preheat the air fryer to 200C/190F.
2. Prepare the sweet potatoes by chopping off the ends and cleaning them. Slice them lengthwise into similar-sized wedges.
3. Drizzle with oil and add seasoning. Toss the sweet potato wedges in the oil and seasoning, ensuring they are all coated.
4. Transfer to the air fryer basket and set the timer for 20 minutes. Check on them at the halfway mark to shake them about.
5. After 20 minutes, they should be crispy on the outside and soft and fluffy on the inside. If they are not, return them to the air fryer and continue cooking, checking on them after 2 minutes.
6. Serve the sweet potato wedges as a side dish or with your favourite dip.
7. NOTES
8. *Sweet Potatoes: if you don't have large sweet potatoes use 2 or 3 mediums ones.

Bacon Twists

 Servings: 8   Cooking Time: 10 Mins.

Ingredients:

- 16 strips of bacon (about 1 lb)

Directions:

1. Twist bacon strips and place in the air fryer basket. Doesn't matter if it's overlapping as the bacon would shrink while cooking
2. Bake 380°F / 194°C for 10 - 12 mins.
3. NOTES
4. No need to flip halfway through cooking time.Bacon crispy some more as it cools.
5. Air fryer temperatures and times may differ depending on manufacturer be sure to read your manual.
6. I do not preheat my air fryer. However when cooking another batch right after the first I start checking the bacon at 7 mins since the air fryer is now preheated.
7. Please refer to body of post for other temperatures to cook your bacon

Fried Cinnamon Sticks

 Servings: 24   Cooking Time: 20 Mins.

Ingredients:

- Peanut oil, for frying
- Skewers
- Cinnamon Bun Dough, see recipe
- Cinnamon Bun Dough:
- Starter:
- 110g caster sugar
- Icing sugar, for topping
- 110g Idaho potato flakes
- 1 tsp. dry active yeast
- 335ml warm-hot tap water
- Cinnamon Buns:
- Nonstick oil spray
- 225g starter
- 110g caster sugar
- 110ml vegetable oil (recommended: Mazola)
- 1 tsp. salt
- 335ml hot tap water
- 1 (1 Tbsp) package active dry yeast
- 1350g all-purpose flour (recommended: Pillsbury)
- Filling:
- 2 sticks butter
- 335g brown sugar, plus more if needed
- 110g ground cinnamon
- 225g chopped pecans
- 110g raisins

Directions:

1. Preheat fryer, or heat oil in large pot to 176 degree C.

2. Cut long 5-cm strips from cinnamon bun dough. Wrap dough around skewers. Place doughnuts into fryer and cook for 4 to 5 minutes, flipping to fry both sides. Place doughnuts aside onto a paper towel lined plate to remove excess oil.

3. Sprinkle with powdered sugar.

4. Buns:

5. When you are ready to bake, preheat the oven to 76 degrees C. Prepare 2 (22.5 by 30-cm) rectangular baking dishes by spraying with nonstick oil spray.

6. In a mixer fitted with a dough hook, mix together starter, caster sugar, vegetable oil, salt, water, yeast and flour.

7. After mixing the dough for about 2 minutes, remove the dough to a bowl sprayed with nonstick oil.

8. Cook's Note: If the dough mix is too loose, add more flour.

9. Cover with a towel and let rise until doubled in size. The rising process will take 1 to 4 hours, depending on the altitude and weather at the time and place you are making the buns.

10. When doubled, dump the whole pile of dough onto a well-floured surface and with a rolling pin manipulate the dough to make a rectangle about 1/4-inch thick.

11. Filling: Melt 2 sticks of butter to where it is creamy and spreadable. Spread the butter onto the dough triangle making sure you spread thoroughly to all corners. Sprinkle brown sugar and then cinnamon

over the butter making sure that the whole triangle is covered, corner to corner. Top with chopped pecans and raisins.

Pizza Rolls

 Servings: 4   Cooking Time: 8 Mins.

Ingredients:

- 240g natural/Greek yoghurt
- 350g self raising flour
- 1 tin/carton of passata/pizza sauce (or enough to cover the dough)
- Grated cheese (your favourite, I like to use Mozzarella)
- 1tsp dried herbs (optional)

Directions:

1. In a bowl, mix together the flour and yoghurt until a dough is formed. If the mixture is too wet and sticky, add in some more flour. If it is too dry, add in a little water. You need to be able to roll out the dough without it sticking or falling about.

2. On a lightly floured work surface roll out the dough into a rectangle.

3. Spread the pizza sauce/passata across the dough. You can use your favourite pizza sauce, or just some regular pasta sauce. Be careful it isn't too runny though or it will just run off the dough. I like to use the Pizza Express pizza sauce cans you can get.

4. Sprinkle your grated cheese over the tomato sauce and add your favourite toppings.

5. Carefully roll the pizza over lengthwise until it is in a sausage shape.

6. Using a sharp knife, or a serrated knife, slice the pizza roll up into even slices.

7. Carefully place the pizza rolls on either a baking tray (if cooking in an oven) or directly to your air fryer basket.

8. Cook at 180C for about 8 minutes, or 12 minutes in an oven. Check on them half way through to make sure they are not cooking too quickly.

Low Carb Mozzarella Sticks

 Servings: 6 Cooking Time: 10 Mins.

Ingredients:

- 12 Mozzarella sticks string cheese, cut in half
- 2 large Eggs beaten
- 1/2 C. Almond flour
- 1/2 C. Parmesan cheese the powdered kind
- 1 tsp. Italian seasoning
- 1/2 tsp. Garlic Salt

Directions:

1. In a bowl combine almond flour, Parmesan cheese, Italian seasoning, and garlic salt.
2. In a separate bowl whisk eggs.
3. One at a time coat your mozzarella stick halves in egg and then toss in the coating mixture. As you finish place them in a resealable container. If you have to make more than 1 layer place parchment paper between the layers of mozzarella sticks.
4. Freeze mozzarella sticks for 30 minutes.
5. Remove from freezer and place in Philips airfryer.
6. Set to 400 degrees F and cook for 5 minutes.
7. Open air fryer and let stand for 1 minute before moving low carb mozzarella sticks to a plate.

Pesto

 Servings: 4 Cooking Time: X Mins.

Ingredients:

- 30g walnuts
- 30g pine nuts
- 3 tsp. chopped garlic (9 cloves)
- 150g fresh basil leaves
- 1 tsp. salt
- 1 tsp. freshly ground black pepper
- 360ml good olive oil
- 100g freshly grated Parmesan

Directions:

1. Place the walnuts, pine nuts and garlic in the bowl of a food processor fitted with a steel blade. Process for 15 seconds.
2. Add the basil leaves, salt and pepper. With the processor running, slowly pour the olive oil into the bowl through the feed tube and process until the pesto is thoroughly pureed.
3. Add the Parmesan and puree for a minute. Use right away, or store the pesto in the refrigerator or freezer with a thin film of olive oil on top.

Air Fryer Mexican Street Corn Recipe

 Servings: 4   Cooking Time: 15 Mins.

Ingredients:

- 4 pieces fresh corn on the cob cleaned
- 1/4 C. crumbled cotija cheese or Feta cheese
- 1/4 tsp. chili powder
- 1/2 tsp. Stone House Seasoning
- 1/4 C. chopped fresh cilantro
- 1 medium lime cut into wedges

Directions:

1. Place corn into the air fryer basket and cook at 390°F for 10 minutes.
2. Sprinkle corn with cheese and cook at 390°F for 5 more minutes.
3. Remove from air fryer and sprinkle with chili powder, Stone House Seasoning, and cilantro. Serve with lime wedges.

Air Fryer Jalapeño Poppers

 Servings: 10   Cooking Time: 5 Mins.

Ingredients:

- 10 Medium jalapeno peppers (Washed)
- 8 oz. cream cheese (room temperature)
- ¼ C. bacon bits
- ¼ C. Shredded cheddar cheese

Directions:

1. Prepare the peppers
2. Cut the peppers in half lengthwise, use a spoon to remove the seeds and membrane. Leave that stem intact. Set peppers aside.
3. Prepare the filling
4. Mix the cream cheese and bacon bits together. Leave out the shredded cheddar cheese.
5. Assemble the poppers
6. Fill each pepper with the cream cheese mixture. Repeat process till all the peppers are stuffed with cream cheese.
7. Top each pepper with some shredded cheddar cheese. Transfer to air fryer basket or tray.
8. Air fry
9. Set temp to 380°F / 180°C and air fry for 5 to 6 mins or until the cheese topping in melted.

How To Cook Frozen Bacon In Air Fryer

 Servings: 8   Cooking Time: 13 Mins.

Ingredients:

- 1 lb. Frozen bacon

Directions:

1. Defrost bacon in air fryer
2. Place frozen bacon in the air fryer basket set temperature to 350°F /177°C and timer to 5 mins.
3. Air fry for 3 mins then flip over bacon with kitchen tongs. Continue cooking for 2 minutes.
4. Separate air fryer thawed bacon
5. Separated the bacon strips using the kitchen tongs
6. Divide thawed bacon strips into two. This will enable you cook in batches.
7. Cook the thawed bacon
8. Place first batch of bacon strips in the air fryer basket. Set temperature to 400°F / 205°C and air fry for 8 to 10 min or until your desired level of crispness. Flip half way through cook time.
9. Repeat for second batch.
10. NOTES
11. Bacon crispy some more as it cools.
12. Air fryer temperatures and times may differ depending on manufacturer be sure to read your manual.
13. I do not preheat my air fryer. However when cooking another batch right after the first I start checking the bacon at 7 mins since the air fryer is now preheated.
14. During the thawing / defrost stage don't be tempted to cook at 400°F it will make the edges get overcooked.

Cinnamon Rolls

 Servings: 8   Cooking Time: 9 Mins.

Ingredients:

- 1 lb. frozen bread dough, thawed
- ¼ C. butter, melted and cooled
- ¾ C. brown sugar
- 1½ tbsp. ground cinnamon,
- CREAM CHEESE GLAZE
- 4 oz. cream cheese, softened
- 2 tbsp. butter, softened
- 1¼ C. powdered sugar
- ½ tsp. vanilla

Directions:

1. Let the bread dough come to room temperature on the counter. On a lightly floured surface roll the dough into a 13-inch by 11-inch rectangle. Position the rectangle so the 13-inch side is facing you. Brush the melted butter all over the dough, leaving a 1-inch border uncovered along the edge farthest away from you.

2. Combine the brown sugar and cinnamon in a small bowl. Sprinkle the mixture evenly over the buttered dough, keeping the 1-inch border uncovered. Roll the dough into a log starting with the edge closest to you. Roll the dough tightly, making sure to roll evenly and push out any air pockets. When you get to the uncovered edge of the dough, press the dough onto the roll to seal it together.

3. Cut the log into 8 pieces, slicing slowly with a sawing motion so you don't flatten the dough. Turn the slices on their sides and cover with a clean kitchen towel. Let the rolls sit in the warmest part of your kitchen for 1½ to 2 hours to rise.

4. To make the glaze, place the cream cheese and butter in a microwave-safe bowl. Soften the mixture in the microwave for 30 seconds at a time until it is easy to stir. Gradually add the powdered sugar and stir to combine. Add the vanilla extract and whisk until smooth. Set aside.

5. When the rolls have risen, pre-heat the air fryer to 350°F.

6. Transfer 4 of the rolls to the air fryer basket. Air-fry for 5 minutes. Turn the rolls over and air-fry for another 4 minutes. Repeat with the remaining 4 rolls.

7. Let the rolls cool for a couple of minutes before glazing. Spread large dollops of cream cheese glaze on top of the warm cinnamon rolls, allowing some of the glaze to drip down the side of the rolls. Serve warm and enjoy!

Dash Air Fryer Lemon Shishito Peppers Recipe

 Servings: 6　　 Cooking Time: 15 Mins.

Ingredients:

- 12 shishito peppers
- 1 tsp. kosher salt
- 2 tsp. vegetable oil
- ½ lemon, chopped into wedges (non-compulsory)

Directions:

1. Adjust the Dash air fryer temperature to 400°F and place 12 shishitos in it.
2. Toss the shishitos with vegetable oil and salt.
3. Fry them for 15 Mins.
4. Squeeze the fresh lemon (cut into wedges) onto shishitos and shake well.
5. Take the lemon shishito peppers out of the air fryer
6. Serve immediately and enjoy.

Air Fryer Chickpeas

 Servings: 1　　 Cooking Time: 15 Mins.

Ingredients:

- 1 x 400g tin chickpeas, drained and rinsed
- 1 tsp. olive oil
- 2 tsp. spice or herb seasoning*

Directions:

1. Drain and rinse the chickpeas.
2. Add the oil and your choice of spices or herbs (see notes).
3. Toss the chickpeas until they are coated in the oil and seasoning.
4. Transfer to the air fryer basket and set off at 200°C (190°F), and air fry for 15 minutes, shaking two or three times.
5. The chickpeas should be hard and crispy when they are ready. If they are still a little soft, air fry them for a few more minutes. Add extra seasoning if required.
6. NOTES
7. *Seasoning
8. You can use any seasoning you like. Suggestions include;
9. Piri Piri
10. Smoked Paprika
11. Garlic Salt
12. Garlic and Herb
13. Mixed Herbs
14. Curry Powder

Air Fryer Sweet Potato Fries

 Servings: 2   Cooking Time: 12 Mins.

Ingredients:

- 1 large sweet potato, approx 350g, (makes 2 small portions, double up for more)
- 1 tsp. rapeseed oil (other oil of your choice, olive, coconut, avocado etc)
- 2 tsp. spice/seasoning mix (ideas include paprika, cayenne, garlic, pepper)
- Salt for seasoning once cooked (optional)

Directions:

1. Preheat the air fryer to 180C (360F) (200C/400F for an oven)
2. Peel the sweet potato (optional).
3. Slice into thin chips.
4. Drizzle with oil, trying to cover as many of the fries as possible.
5. Sprinkle the spice mix over the fries and toss to coat.
6. Lay prepared fries in the air fryer basket (or on parchment paper on a baking tray if using an oven)
7. Cook for 12 minutes, (15 to 20 minutes in an oven), checking halfway to shake about/turn over.NOTES
8. Remember different air fryer models can cook at different speeds. Until you are familiar with your air fryer, make sure you check on the food frequently to make sure it isn't over cooking.
9. If the fries aren't crisping up, try to spread them out a bit so that they are not over lapping each other. You can also spray with a little more oil.

Air Fryer Biscuits

 Servings: 9   Cooking Time: 10 Mins.

Ingredients:

- 1 C. almond flour
- 1/2 tsp. baking powder
- 1/4 tsp. pink himalayan salt
- 1 C. shredded cheddar cheese

- 2 large eggs
- 2 tsp. butter, melted
- 2 tsp. sour cream

Directions:

1. Combine the almond flour, baking powder, and salt in a large bowl. Mix in the cheddar cheese by hand until well combined.

2. Add eggs, butter, and sour cream to the center and blend with a large fork, spoon, or your hands, until a sticky batter forms.

3. Fit a piece of parchment paper into your air fryer basket. Drop ¼ cup-sized (for large) or 2 tablespoon-sized (for small) portions of batter onto the parchment.

4. Air Fry/"Bake" at 400 degrees F for 6 minutes (for small) to 10 minutes (for large), until golden brown and cooked through. Repeat with remaining batter as needed. Serve immediately!

5. Note: recipe can yield 9 small biscuits or 5 large biscuits. Nutrition is for 9 small biscuits.

6. Alternatively, you could place the batter in silicone muffin liners and air fry them for taller biscuits (yields 7-9, bakes 10-12 minutes depending on how much you fill them).

Bacon Pineapple Appetizer In The Air Fryer

 Servings: 12   Cooking Time: 10 Mins.

Ingredients:

- 1 pineapple
- 1 lb. bacon

- 1/2 C. brown sugar optional

Directions:

1. Cut the pineapple into cubes.

2. Roll and cover the pineapple in brown sugar if desired.

3. Wrap the pineapple in bacon and secure with a toothpick.

4. Place in a lightly sprayed air fryer basket and repeat for remaining pineapple chunks.

5. Cook at 400°F/200°C for 10 minutes, flipping at the halfway point.

Vegetables & Vegetarian Recipes

Air Fryer Falafel Recipe

 Servings: 4   Cooking Time: 30 Mins.

Ingredients:

- 8 oz. dried chickpeas (1 1/3 cups)
- 1/4 tsp. baking soda
- 1 C. fresh parsley leaves and tender stems
- 1 C. fresh cilantro leaves and tender stems
- 1 small shallot
- 2 cloves garlic
- 3 tbsp. olive oil
- 2 tsp. kosher salt
- 1 1/2 tsp. ground cumin
- 1/2 tsp. baking powder
- 1/8 tsp. cayenne pepper (optional)
- 1 to 4 tbsp. all-purpose or chickpea flour (if needed)
- Cooking spray

Directions:

1. Place 8 oz. dried chickpeas and 1/4 tsp. baking soda in a large bowl and cover with a few inches of cold water. Let sit at cool room temperature at least 18 and up to 24 hours. Drain, rinse with fresh water, and drain well again.

2. Coarsely chop 1 small shallot and 2 garlic cloves and add to the bowl of a food processor fit with a blade attachment. Add the chickpeas, 1 C. fresh parsley leaves and tender stems, 1 C. fresh cilantro leaves and tender stems, 3 tbsp. olive oil, 2 tsp. kosher salt, 1 1/2 tsp. ground cumin, 1/2 tsp. baking powder, and 1/8 tsp. cayenne pepper. Pulse for 10 seconds, then scrape down the sides with a rubber spatula.

3. Repeat pulsing and scraping 2 to 3 more times ,until the mixture comes together and the chickpeas are broken down but haven't lost all of their texture. If the mixture isn't coming together, gradually pulse in all-purpose or chickpea flour 1 tbsp. at a time. Transfer the mixture to a bowl and refrigerate for at least 30 minutes.

4. Heat the air fryer to 350°F.

5. Lightly coat an air fryer basket with cooking spray. Using a tbsp. or a small cookie scoop, scoop the mixture into damp hands and roll into balls. Cook in 2 batches: place the falafel in the basket in a single layer. Air fry for 10 minutes. Flip and air fry until golden-brown, about 5 minutes more.

6. Serve the falafel with a dipping sauce or build a sandwich in a warmed pita. The falafel are best eaten immediately.

Air Fryer Herbed Brussels Sprouts

 Servings: 4   Cooking Time: 8 Mins.

Ingredients:

- 1 lb. brussels sprouts (cleaned and trimmed)
- ½ tsp. dried thyme
- 1 tsp. dried parsley
- 1 tsp. garlic powder (Or 4 cloves, minced)
- ¼ tsp. salt
- 2 tsp. oil

Directions:

1. Remove any outer leaves of the brussels sprouts that don't look healthy. Blanch your brussels sprouts, either by boiling them for 13-15 minutes or by microwaving them on high for about 3-4 minutes.

2. Trim the brussels sprouts and cut them in half.

3. Place all ingredients in a medium or large mixing bowl and toss to coat the brussels sprouts evenly.

4. Pour them into the food basket of the air fryer and close it up.

5. Set the heat to 390 F. and the time to 8 minutes. This setting roasts them nicely on the outside while leaving the insides a nicely cooked al dente.

6. Cool slightly and serve.

7. NOTES

8. Please note that the nutrition data below is a ballpark figure. Exact data is not possible.

Air Roasted Asparagus

 Servings: 4   Cooking Time: 10 Mins.

Ingredients:

- 1 lb. fresh asparagus , ends trimmed
- 1-2 tsp. olive oil
- salt , to taste
- black pepper , to taste

Directions:

1. Wash and trim the tough ends of your asparagus. Coat asparagus with olive oil and season with salt and pepper. Add extra spices if you want. Make sure to coat the asparagus tips so they don't burn or dry out too fast.

2. Air Fry at 380°F for 7-10 minutes, depending on thickness, shake and turn asparagus halfway through cooking.

3. Let it cool a bit and taste for seasoning & tenderness. Cook for an extra minute or two if desired and season with extra salt and pepper if needed.

Air Fryer Squash Soup

 Servings: 4   Cooking Time: 45 Mins.

Ingredients:

- 2 1/2 lb. Butternut squash, peeled, cut into 1-inch pieces
- 2 medium carrots, cut into 1-inch pieces
- 1 large onion, cut into 1/2-inch-thick wedges
- 4 cloves garlic, 2 whole and 2 thinly sliced, divided
- 1 Fresno chile, seeded
- 4 sprigs fresh thyme
- 4 tbsp. Olive oil, divided
- Kosher salt
- 2 tbsp. Pepitas
- 1/4 tsp. Smoked paprika
- Sour cream and crusty bread, for serving

Directions:

1. In large bowl, toss squash, carrots, onion, whole garlic cloves, chile, thyme, 2 tbsp. oil and 3/4 tsp. salt. Transfer to air-fryer basket and air-fry at 400°F, shaking basket occasionally, until vegetables are tender, 30 minutes. Discard thyme sprigs.

2. Meanwhile, in small skillet on medium, cook sliced garlic in remaining 2 tbsp. oil, stirring, until garlic begins to lightly brown around the edges, 2 minutes. Add pepitas and paprika and a pinch of salt and cook 1 minute; transfer to a bowl.

3. Transfer all but 1/2 C. squash to blender, add 1 C. water and puree, gradually adding 3 more C. water, pureeing until smooth. Reheat if necessary and serve topped with sour cream and spiced pepitas and with crusty bread if desired. Serve topped with remaining squash.

Trader Joes Frozen Handsome Cut Potato Fries In The Air Fryer

 Servings: 8   Cooking Time: 17 Mins.

Ingredients:

- 24 oz. (425 g) Trader Joes Frozen Handsome Cut Potato Fries
- Kosher salt or sea salt , to taste
- ground black pepper , to taste (optional)

Directions:

1. Place the frozen fries in air fryer basket and spread them evenly over the basket. If you have a large air fryer, you can cook a whole bag at a time. Otherwise just cook a half a bag per batch for best results. A single layer is best and two layers deep is about the max you should do. You don't need thaw them first or to spray any extra oil.

2. Air fry the frozen fries at 400°F/205°C for about 12-17 minutes. About halfway through cooking, shake the basket and gently turn the fries. Try not to break them. For crisper, evenly cooked fries, turn them multiples times while cooking.

3. If needed, Air Fry for additional 1-3 minutes to crisp to your preferred liking. Season with salt and pepper if desired.

4. NOTES

5. No Oil Necessary. Cook Fries Frozen – Do not thaw first.

6. Shake several times for even cooking & Don't overcrowd fryer basket.

7. If cooking in multiple batches, the first batch will take longer to cook if Air Fryer is not already pre-heated.

8. Recipes were cooked in 3-4 qt air fryers. If using a larger air fryer, the recipe might cook quicker so adjust cooking time.

9. Remember to set a timer to shake/flip/toss the food as directed in recipe.

Air Fryer 2-ingredient Sweet Potato Rolls

 Servings: 6 　　　 🕐 Cooking Time: 14 Mins.

Ingredients:

- 1 C. (240 ml) cooked sweet potato , mashed
- 1 C. (240 ml) self rising flour
- oil spray , for basket & rolls

Directions:

1. In bowl, combine sweet potato and flour. Stir with a fork until a dough ball forms. Make sure to scrape all the flour and sweet potato along the sides of the bowl.

2. On a lightly floured surface, knead the soft dough ball for about 1 minute, or until smooth. Don't keep adding too much flour to the dough or else it will be tough and hard. You want to keep the dough soft and pliable, so don't over-knead it.

3. Cut the dough into 6 equal pieces. Roll the dough between your hands to form 6 balls. Let the dough balls rest for about 30 minutes (they will also rise slightly).

4. Spray air fryer basket or tray with oil. Gently place dough balls in the basket, evenly spaced apart. Lightly spray the tops of the dough balls with oil.

5. Air Fry at 330°F/165°C for 10-14 minutes or until the rolls are cooked through. Allow to cool and serve with butter or as small slider or sandwich buns.

Crispy Air Fryer Baked Potatoes

 Servings: 2 　　　 🕐 Cooking Time: 40-50 Mins.

Ingredients:

- 2 medium russet potatoes (8 to 10 oz. each)
- 1 tsp. neutral oil, such as peanut or vegetable
- 1/2 tsp. kosher salt, plus more for serving
- Butter and freshly ground black pepper, for serving

Directions:

1. Heat the air fryer to 375°F for at least 10 minutes. Meanwhile, rinse, scrub, and dry 2 medium russet potatoes. Use a fork to prick the potatoes in a few places. Drizzle the potatoes with 1 tsp. neutral oil and rub with your hands to coat the potatoes. Season the potatoes with 1/2 tsp. kosher salt.

2. Place the potatoes in the preheated air fryer. Roast until the potatoes can be easily pierced with a paring knife, about 40 minutes. Remove the potatoes from the air fryer with tongs, then cut each one lengthwise to split. Serve with butter, salt, and pepper, or as desired.

Easy Air Fryer Jalapeno Poppers

 Servings: 5   Cooking Time: 5 Mins.

Ingredients:

- 10 fresh jalapenos
- 6 oz. cream cheese I used reduced-fat
- 1/4 C. shredded cheddar cheese
- 2 slices bacon cooked and crumbled
- cooking oil spray

Directions:

1. Slice the jalapenos in half, vertically, to create 2 halves per jalapeno.
2. Place the cream cheese in a bowl. Microwave for 15 seconds to soften.
3. Remove the seeds and the inside of the jalapeno. (Save some of the seeds if you prefer spicy poppers)
4. Combine the cream cheese, crumbled bacon, and shredded cheese in a bowl. Mix well.
5. For extra spicy poppers, add some of the seeds as noted above to the cream cheese mixture, and mix well.
6. Stuff each of the jalapenos with the cream cheese mixture.
7. Load the poppers into the Air Fryer. Spray the poppers with cooking oil.
8. Close the Air Fryer. Cook the poppers on 370 degrees for 5 minutes to 8 minutes.
9. Remove from the Air Fryer and cool before serving.
10. NOTES
11. Use your judgment to determine how long you want your poppers to cook. If you prefer for your poppers to have a crunch, 5-8 minutes is optimal cook time. For softer jalapenos, cook for 10 minutes.
12. I did not add any salt and pepper to this recipe because I feel like the bacon provides enough flavor. Feel free to add salt and pepper if you wish.

Air Fryer Hamburger Hamlet Zucchini Zircles

 Servings: 3   Cooking Time: 8 Mins.

Ingredients:

- 3 large Zucchini
- 3/4 C. Milk
- 1/2 C. All Purpose Flour
- 1 C. Seasoned Dry Italian Breadcrumbs
- 1/2 C. Powdered Sugar
- 1 C. Hamburger Hamlet's Secret Apricot Sauce
- Tools
- Oil Mister
- 1 Half Cookie Sheet
- 1 Wire Baking Rack

Directions:

1. Line a Cookie Sheet with Paper Towels. Wash and dry Zucchini. Cut Zucchini about 1/4 inch thick, like Poker Chips and place on lined Cookie Sheet.

2. Line up three shallow bowls, placing flour in one, milk in the next and Seasoned Bread Crumbs in the third. With one dry hand, coat Zucchini in flour, shake off excess and drop into milk. Sink/flip with a fork and then place Zucchini in bowl with Breadcrumbs.. With other dry hand, thoroughly coat Zucchini and place onto Wire Baking Rack.

3. In a single layer, gently place Zucchini Zircles in prepared/greased Air Fryer Basket and use an Oil Mister to spray well with Oil.

4. Cook at 390 degrees for 8 minutes, carefully flipping one-half way through.

5. Remove from Air Fryer and sprinkle with Powdered Sugar. Serve with Hamburger Hamlet's Secret Apricot Sauce.

Air Fryer Frozen Jalapeño Poppers

 Servings: 2   Cooking Time: 8 Mins.

Ingredients:

- 6 Frozen Jalapeño Poppers

Directions:

1. Place the frozen jalapeño poppers in the air fryer basket and spread out evenly in a single layer. No oil spray is needed.

2. Air Fry at 380°F/193°C for 5 minutes. Gently shake or turn. Continue to Air Fry at 380°F/193°C for another 2-4 minutes or until the cheese just starts to ooze out.

3. Make sure to let them cool a little before eating. The filling can be super hot.

4. NOTES

5. based on using Frozen Cauliflower Veggie Tots.

6. Air Frying Tips and Notes

7. No Oil Necessary. Cook Frozen – Do not thaw first.

8. Shake or turn if needed. Don't overcrowd the air fryer basket.

9. Recipe timing is based on a non-preheated air fryer. If cooking in multiple batches back to back, the following batches may cook a little quicker.

10. Recipes were tested in 3.7 to 6 qt. air fryers. If using a larger air fryer, they might cook quicker so adjust cooking time.

11. Remember to set a timer to shake/flip/toss as directed in recipe.

Crispy Air Fryer Roasted Brussels Sprouts

 Servings: 4   Cooking Time: 15 Mins.

Ingredients:

- 1 lb. (454 g) brussels sprouts , ends removed and cut into bite-sized pieces
- 3 tbsp. (15 ml) olive oil , or less if you have less brussels sprouts
- 1 tbsp. (15 ml) balsamic vinegar
- kosher salt , to taste
- black pepper , to taste

Directions:

1. Add brussels sprouts in a large bowl. Evenly drizzle oil and balsamic vinegar over brussels sprouts. Add salt & pepper to taste. Toss the brussels sprouts well to completely coat with the oil and balsamic vinegar. Make sure to toss well to coat all the brussels sprouts. There shouldn't be any liquid left pooling at the bottom of the bowl.

2. Gently add the brussels sprouts to the air fryer basket or rack. Air fry at 360°F for about 15-20 minutes, depending on size of brussels sprouts. Shake and gently stir half way through, about 8 minutes into cooking. Make sure you shake at the halfway mark! You don't want to end up with uneven cooking. Continue to air fry the brussels for the remainder of the time, or until the brussels are golden brown and cooked through.

3. TIP: Check earlier if needed to make sure brussels sprouts don't burn or shake/toss more often for even cooking (about 3 times). Or cook a little longer if needed to get everything crispy .

4. Season with extra salt and pepper if needed on the brussels sprouts. Well seasoned brussels are extra tasty. Enjoy!

5. NOTES

6. Don't crowd the basket. It's better to cook in multiple smaller batches for even cooking, than it is to cook in one large batch.

7. Doubling the recipe will work great but make sure your air fryer is large enough. We used a 3.7 qt for 1 lb. of brussels sprouts. You might need add an additional 1-2 minutes of cooking time and give an extra shake or two while cooking. If using a larger air fryer, the recipe might cook quicker so adjust cooking time.

8. If cooking in multiple batches, the first batch will take longer to cook if Air Fryer is not already pre-heated.

9. Remember to set a timer to shake/flip/toss the food as directed in recipe.

Breaded Mushrooms

 Servings: X   Cooking Time: X Mins.

Ingredients:

- 250 grams Button mushrooms
- flour
- 1 egg
- Breadcrumbs
- 80 grams Finely grated Parmigiano Reggiano cheese
- salt and pepper

Directions:

1. In a bowl, mix the breadcrumbs with the Parmigiano cheese and place to one side.

2. In a separate bowl, beat an egg and place to one side.

3. Pat dry the mushrooms with kitchen paper.

4. Roll the mushrooms in the flour.

5. Dip the mushrooms in the egg.

6. Dip the mushrooms in the breadcrumbs/cheese mixture ensuring an even coating.

7. Cook in the Airfryer on 180 degrees for 7 minutes. Shake once whilst cooking.

8. Serve warm with your favourite dipping sauce.

Ultra Crispy Air Fryer Chickpeas

 Servings: 4   Cooking Time: 15 Mins.

Ingredients:

- 19 oz. can of chickpeas (drained and rinsed)
- 1 tbsp. olive oil
- 1/8 tsp. salt
- 1/4 tsp. garlic powder
- 1/4 tsp. onion powder
- 1/2 tsp. paprika
- 1/4 tsp. cayenne (optional)

Directions:

1. Heat air fryer to 390°F / 200°C.

2. Drain and rinse chickpeas (no need to dry). Toss with olive oil and spices.

3. Dump the whole batch of chickpeas in the air fryer basket. Cook for 12-15 minutes, shaking a couple of times.

4. When chickpeas are cooked to your liking, remove from air fryer, taste and add more salt and pepper to taste.

5. Store in an open container.

Air Fryer Baked Sweet Potatoes

 Servings: 3 Cooking Time: 40 Mins.

Ingredients:

- 3 medium sweet potatoes
- 1 tsp. olive oil
- 1/2 tsp. kosher salt
- Toppings (Optional)
- 3 tsp. butter
- 1 1/2 tsp. cinnamon
- 1 1/2 tsp. brown sugar

Directions:

1. Preheat the air fryer to 390 degrees Fahrenheit and prepare the air fryer basket.
2. Wash and clean the sweet potatoes.
3. Cover the sweet potatoes with the olive oil. Take a fork and lightly prick the skin all over for each of the sweet potatoes.
4. Cover the sweet potatoes with kosher salt.
5. Place the sweet potatoes in a single layer in the basket of the air fryer. Cook on 390 degrees Fahrenheit for 40-45 minutes.
6. Carefully remove the sweet potatoes from the air fryer basket.
7. Slice open the sweet cooked potatoes, fluff the sweet potato flesh, and top with butter, cinnamon, and brown sugar. Serve.

Air Fryer Garlic Zucchini

 Servings: 2 Cooking Time: 15 Mins.

Ingredients:

- 2 zucchini (@ 1 lb. or 455g total)
- Olive oil or cooking spray
- 1 tsp. (5 g) garlic powder
- salt , to taste
- black pepper , to taste

Directions:

1. Wash and dry the zucchini. Cut the ends of the zucchini, if desired. Cut the zucchini into 1/2" thick slices (either into lengthwise slices or into coins). If cutting into lengthwise slices, cut to length to fit the width of your air fryer basket if needed.
2. Lightly oil or spray the zucchini slices on both sides and then season with garlic powder, salt and pepper.
3. Air Fry at 400°F for 8-14 minutes or until browned and cooked through.

Favorite Air Fryer Recipes

Air Fryer Ham And Cheese Turnovers

 Servings: 4 Cooking Time: 10 Mins.

Ingredients:

- 1 tube (13.8 ounces) refrigerated pizza crust
- 1/4 lb. thinly sliced black forest deli ham
- 1 medium pear, thinly sliced and divided
- 1/4 C. chopped walnuts, toasted
- 2 tbsp. crumbled blue cheese

Directions:

1. Preheat air fryer to 400°. On a lightly floured surface, unroll pizza crust into a 12-in. square. Cut into 4 squares. Layer ham, half of pear slices, walnuts and blue cheese diagonally over half of each square to within 1/2 in. of edges. Fold 1 corner over filling to the opposite corner, forming a triangle; press edges with a fork to seal.

2. In batches, arrange turnovers in a single layer on greased tray in air-fryer basket; spritz with cooking spray. Cook until golden brown, 4-6 minutes on each side. Garnish with remaining pear slices.

Air Fryer Kielbasa

 Servings: 4 Cooking Time: 8 Mins.

Ingredients:

- 1 Rope Smoked Kielbasa sausage (or cut into even slices)
- Serving suggestions
- ¼ C. Ketchup or Barbecue sauce (substitute with your favorite dipping sauce)
- Scrambled eggs
- Potatoes and peppers.

Directions:

1. cooking the whole rope of sausage
2. Place sausage rope in air fryer basket and set temperature to 380F / 190C and cook for 4 mins then flip over with a pair of kitchen tongs and cook for another 5 minutes.
3. for sliced Kielbasa
4. Place sausage slices in the air fryer and air fry at 380F / 190C for 4 mins then shake the basket and continue cooking for 3 to 4 mins or until you reach your desired level or browned.

Air Fryer Pizza Recipe

 Servings: 4-6   Cooking Time: 1 Hour 20-36 Mins.

Ingredients:

- 1 lb. pizza dough, thawed if frozen
- Cooking spray
- 1 C. prepared pizza sauce
- 2 2/3 C. shredded Italian cheese blend
- Topping options:
- Pepperoni
- Sliced mushrooms
- Sliced peppers

Directions:

1. Divide 1 lb. pizza dough into 8 (2-ounce) pieces. If refrigerated, let sit on the counter until room temperature, at least 30 minutes.

2. Heat an air fryer to 375°F.

3. Press each piece of pizza dough into a round up to 6 1/2-inches wide, or 1/2 inch smaller than the size of your air fryer basket.

4. Coat the air fryer basket with cooking spray and carefully transfer one round of dough into the basket. (The basket will be warm.) Gently press the dough to the edges of the basket without touching the sides. Spread 2 tbsp. pizza sauce onto the dough, then sprinkle with 1/3 C. of the shredded cheese and top with any desired toppings.

5. Air fry until the crust is golden-brown and the cheese is melted, 10 to 12 minutes.

6. Carefully lift the pizza out of the air fryer basket with tongs or a spatula. Place on a cutting board and cut into wedges. Serve immediately and repeat with the remaining dough and toppings.

Air Fryer Frozen Taquitos

 Servings: 4   Cooking Time: 10 Mins.

Ingredients:

- 8 Frozen Taquitos
- oil spray , to coat the taquitos

Directions:

1. Place the frozen taquitos in the air fryer basket and spread out into a single even layer. Coat the taquitos evenly with oil spray.

2. Air Fry at 380°F/195°C for 7-10 minutes or until crispy to your liking, gently shaking and turning the taquitos halfway through cooking.

3. NOTES

4. Air Frying Tips and Notes:

5. Cook Frozen – Do not thaw first.

6. Shake or turn as needed. Don't overcrowd the air fryer basket.

7. Recipe timing is based on a non-preheated air fryer. If cooking in multiple batches back to back, the following batches may cook a little quicker.

8. Recipes were tested in 3.7 to 6 qt. air fryers. If using a larger air fryer, they might cook quicker so adjust cooking time.

9. Remember to set a timer to shake/flip/toss as directed in recipe.

Air Fryer Bbq Little Smokies

Servings: 5 **Cooking Time: 10 Mins.**

Ingredients:

- 12 oz. Lit'l Smokies
- 1/4 C. BBQ sauce
- 2 tsp. brown sugar

Directions:

1. Add the Lit'l Smokies to the prepared air fryer basket and cook at 350 degrees Fahrenheit for 6 minutes. Toss halfway through.

2. Brush the Lit'l smokies with BBQ sauce and then sprinkle the brown sugar over the top. Cook for an additional 2-3 minutes.

3. Carefully remove the sausages from the air fryer and serve.

Rachel Khoo's Pan-fried Dumplings

 Servings: 4   Cooking Time: 10 Mins.

Ingredients:

- For the dough
- 250g plain white flour, plus extra for dusting
- 180ml just boiled water
- 2 tsp. vegetable oil
- 150ml water
- For the filling
- 200g leftover sunday roast (approx. 150g meat and 50g vegetables is my ideal combo)
- 50g baby spinach
- 50g mature hard goat's cheese or Parmesan cheese, finely grated

- Spring onions, sliced at an angle to serve (optional)
- Sriracha or soy (optional) or other chili sauce
- Equipment
- Grater
- Bowl
- 5cm crimped biscuit cutter (or a glass)
- Large non-stick pan with lid
- Freezer bag
- Rolling pin

Directions:

1. Tip the flour into a bowl and make a well in the centre. Pour in the just boiled water and stir together till you have a very crumbly, lumpy dough. Knead until it comes together into a ball. If the dough is very dry add a tbsp. of water. Transfer the dough to a flour-dusted work surface and knead for about 5 minutes until the dough is smooth and springs back when touched.

2. Roll the dough in a little flour and place it in a freezer bag. Seal the bag and leave it to rest at room temperature for at least 15 minutes. Prepare the filling. Finely chop the leftover Sunday roastand spinachand mix together with the grated cheese.

3. Lightly dust the work surface and a large plate with flour. Divide the rested dough into quarters. roll one quarter into a long rectangle about 5cm wide and 3mm thick. Place a heaped tsp. of the filling 2.5cm from the end and fold the end over to coverthe filling. Press down firmly, making sure to press out any air pockets. Use the biscuit cutter to cut out a half-moon shape and trim the excess pastry. Place the ravioli on the plate dusted with flour. Repeat with the rest of the dough and filling, squeezing together the leftover bits of dough and rerolling.

4. Heat the oil in a large non-stick pan until smoking hot, then add the ravioli in batches. Turn down the heat and cook for 2 minutes or until the base of each is golden. Add 150ml water, cover with the lid and cook for 8 minutes until the water evaporates. Serve immediately.

Air-fryer Ravioli

 Servings: 1-1/2 Cooking Time: 10 Mins.

Ingredients:

- 1 C. seasoned bread crumbs
- 1/4 C. shredded Parmesan cheese
- 2 tsp. dried basil
- 1/2 C. all-purpose flour
- 2 large eggs, lightly beaten
- 1 package (9 ounces) frozen beef ravioli, thawed
- Cooking spray
- Fresh minced basil, optional
- 1 C. Bertolli d'Italia Marinara Sauce, warmed

Directions:

1. Preheat air fryer to 350°. In a shallow bowl, mix bread crumbs, Parmesan cheese and basil. Place flour and eggs in separate shallow bowls. Dip ravioli in flour to coat both sides; shake off excess. Dip in eggs, then in crumb mixture, patting to help coating adhere.

2. In batches, arrange ravioli in a single layer on greased tray in air-fryer basket; spritz with cooking spray. Cook until golden brown, 3-4 minutes. Turn; spritz with cooking spray. Cook until golden brown, 3-4 minutes longer. If desired, immediately sprinkle with basil and additional Parmesan cheese. Serve warm with marinara sauce.

Air Fryer 6 Minute Pita Bread Cheese Pizza

 Servings: X   Cooking Time: 6 Mins.

Ingredients:

- 1 Pita Bread
- 1 tbsp. Pizza Sauce
- 1/4 C. Mozarella Cheese
- 1 drizzle Extra Virgin Olive Oil
- 1 Stainless Steel Short Legged Trivet
- Toppings
- 7 slices Pepperoni or more
- 1/4 C. Sausage
- 1 tbsp. Yellow/Brown Onion sliced thin
- 1/2 tsp. Fresh Garlic minced

Directions:

1. Use a spoon and swirl Pizza Sauce on to Pita Bread. Add your favorite toppings and Cheese. Add a little drizzle of Extra Virgin Olive Oil over top of Pizza.

2. Place in Air Fryer and place a Trivet over Pita Bread. Cook at 350 degrees for 6 minutes. Carefully remove from Air Fryer and cut.

Basil Pesto

 Servings: X   Cooking Time: X Mins.

Ingredients:

- 2 C. packed fresh basil leaves
- 2 cloves garlic
- 1/4 C. pine nuts
- 2/3 C. extra-virgin olive oil, divided
- Salt and freshly ground black pepper, to taste
- 1/2 C. freshly grated Pecorino cheese

Directions:

1. Combine the basil, garlic, and pine nuts in a food processor and pulse until coarsely chopped. Add 1/2 C. of the oil and process until fully incorporated and smooth. Season with salt and pepper.

2. If using immediately, add all the remaining oil and pulse until smooth. Transfer the pesto to a large serving bowl and mix in the cheese.

3. If freezing, transfer to an air-tight container and drizzle remaining oil over the top. Freeze for up to 3 months. Thaw and stir in cheese.

Air Fryer Frozen Pizza Rolls

 Servings: 3   Cooking Time: 10 Mins.

Ingredients:

- 18 (170 g) Frozen Pizza Rolls

Directions:

1. Place the pizza rolls in the air fryer basket and spread out in to a single even layer. Don't overcrowd the basket or else they won't cook evenly. No oil spray is needed.

2. For Regular Sized Pizza Rolls: Air Fry at 380°F/193°C for 6-10 minutes or until golden and nearly starting to ooze their filling. Shake and flip over about halfway through cooking.

3. For Mini Sized Pizza Rolls: Air Fry at 380°F/193°C for 5-8 minutes or until golden and nearly starting to ooze their filling. Shake and flip over about halfway through cooking.

4. Let them rest for a couple minutes to cool off so the filling isn't dangerously hot. Be careful with that first bite!

5. NOTES

6. Air Frying Tips and Notes:

7. No Oil Necessary. Cook Frozen – Do not thaw first.

8. Shake or turn if needed. Don't overcrowd the air fryer basket.

9. Recipe timing is based on a non-preheated air fryer. If cooking in multiple batches of pizza rolls back to back, the following batches may cook a little quicker.

10. Recipes were tested in 3.7 to 6 qt. air fryers. If using a larger air fryer, the pizza rolls might cook quicker so adjust cooking time.

11. Remember to set a timer to shake/flip/toss as directed in recipe.

Air Fryer Pizza Rolls

 Servings: 4   Cooking Time: 6 Mins.

Ingredients:

- Homemade Pizza Rolls
- 1 pizza dough Pillsbury Thin Crust
- 1/2 C. mozzarella cheese shredded
- 1/2 C. pizza sauce pizza sauce or marinara sauce
- 1 egg
- 1/4 C. pepperonis cut into small pieces
- 1 tsp. water
- Frozen Totino's Pizza Rolls
- 20 pizza rolls Totino's brand is my favorite

Directions:

1. Homemade Pizza Rolls
2. Roll out the pizza dough and use a large cookie cutter to create 5" circles.
3. Add a tbsp. of pizza sauce to the middle of the dough.
4. Sprinkle mozzarella cheese, pepperonis, and additional toppings on the pizza sauce. Careful to not overfill the rolls.
5. Whisk the egg and water together. Use a brush to brush the inner edges of the dough. Fold over the dough and then press down to seal the edges. Use a fork to seal the edges completely. Continue with the remainder of the pizza rolls.
6. Place the pizza rolls into the prepared Air Fryer basket. Prepare the basket with nonstick spray or with parchment paper. Line the basket with the pizza rolls in a single layer. Air fry the pizza rolls on 350 degrees Fahrenheit for 6-8 minutes, flipping halfway through.
7. Serve with extra pizza sauce or marinara sauce for dipping.
8. Frozen Totino's Pizza Rolls
9. Preheat the air fryer to 380 degrees Fahrenheit.
10. Add the pizza rolls to the bottom of the basket and set the cook time for 6 minutes. Flip the pizza rolls halfway at the 3 minute mark.
11. Set the pizza rolls to the side for 2 minutes before serving, they're HOT.

Air Fryer Hamburgers

Servings: 4 **Cooking Time: 12 Mins.**

Ingredients:

- 4 hamburger patties

Directions:

1. Preheat the Air Fryer to 370 degrees Fahrenheit. Prepare the Air Fryer basket with nonstick cooking spray.

2. Add the hamburger patties into the Air Fryer basket in a single layer.

3. Cook in the preheated fryer for 6 minutes. Flip the hamburger patties and cook for an additional 5-7 minutes, depending on how well done you would like the hamburgers.

4. Carefully remove the hamburger patties from the Air Fryer basket and serve with your favorite sides and toppings.

Air Fryer Pepperoni Pizza Egg Rolls

 Servings: 15   Cooking Time: 30 Mins.

Ingredients:

- 4 oz. (113 g) pepperoni slices , chopped
- 1 C. (112 g) shredded mozzarella cheese
- 1/2 C. (120 ml) marinara sauce , plus extra for dipping
- 1 tsp. (5 ml) dried Italian seasoning (or any combination of dried basil, oregano, thyme, rosemary, etc.)
- 1/2 C. (75 g) bell peppers , chopped
- 15 (15) egg roll wrappers
- water , for sealing the wrappers
- oil spray , for coating the egg rolls
- 1/2-1 C. (120-240 ml) optional dipping sauce of choice , marinara, ranch, bbq sauce, etc.

Directions:

1. Add pepperoni, mozzarella cheese, sauce, Italian seasonings and bell peppers in bowl. Mix well.

2. Using egg roll wrappers or spring roll wrappers, add about 2 tbsp. of the filling to each wrapper. Tuck and roll the wrapper around the filling (watch the video in the post above to see how to roll even and tight rolls). Brush the top corner of the wrapper with water to help seal the wrapper end, and then finish rolling the egg roll. Repeat for all the egg rolls.

3. Brush or spray rolls with oil to coat. Place a single layer of egg rolls in the air fryer basket (cook in batches).

4. Air Fry 380°F for 12-16 minutes, flipping halfway through. Cook until the wrapper is crispy and browned. If you use the larger wrapper or if your wrappers are thicker cook a little longer so that all the layers can cook through to avoid being tough and chewy.

5. Allow to cool a little (the filling will be super hot right after cooking), and then serve with your favorite dipping sauce.

Air Fryer Hot Dogs

 Servings: 4   Cooking Time: 10 Mins.

Ingredients:

- 4 hot dog buns
- 4 hot dogs
- oil spray , for coating hot dogs
- FOR SERVING
- ketchup , mustard, BBQ sauce, pickles, jalapeños, sauteed onion, etc.

Directions:

1. Lightly spray hot dogs with oil spray. Place in air fryer basket or air fryer rack.

2. Air Fry at 380°F for 8-10 minutes depending on your preferred texture and size of hot dogs. If you like your hot dogs extra crispy (similar to grilled hot dogs), Air Fry at 400°F for about 6-8 minutes. Flip the hot dogs half way through cooking.

3. Place hot dogs in the buns and cook in the air fryer for about one more minute for the buns to warm and crisp. Or warm the buns separately. Serve with your favorite toppings!

4. One note about the hot dogs: they are sold in differnet sizes and lenghts! So after you cook your first batch, you'll know exactly how long to cook your future batches in the air fryer.

Cosori Air Fryer Baked Potted Egg Recipe

 Servings: 3   Cooking Time: 14 Mins.

Ingredients:

- 3 eggs
- 1/3 C. heavy cream
- 6 slices streaky bacon, smoked & diced
- 3 tsp. grated Parmesan cheese
- 2 C. washed baby spinach
- Salt & pepper to taste
- Nonstick cooking spray

Directions:

1. Choose Preheat on your Cosori air fryer. Switch the heating to 350°F and tap Start/Pause button
2. Toss the nonstick cooking spray with three 3-inch ramekins
3. Add an egg to each ramekin after greasing with nonstick cooking spray
4. Heat the bacon in a pan for about 5 minutes, or until crispy
5. Combine the bacon with Parmesan and heavy cream, and continue cooking for 2 more Mins.
6. Spread the cream mixture evenly (and generously) on top of the eggs
7. Transfer the ramekins into the preheated Cosori air fryer. Cook at 350°F for 4 minutes, or until the egg white is fully set
8. Season with salt and pepper to taste and enjoy while still warm

Printed in Great Britain
by Amazon

19864173R10059